Women in Physical Education

Department of Hygiene and Physical Edu. Wellesley College

## Amy Morris Nomans at 80

# WOMEN IN PHYSICAL EDUCATION:

## THEIR ROLE IN WORK, HOME, AND HISTORY

*by Elizabeth Halsey*

G. P. Putnam's Sons   New York

GV
211
,H3

Copyright © 1961 by G. P. PUTNAM'S SONS

Library of Congress Catalog Number: 61-5720

MANUFACTURED IN THE UNITED STATES OF AMERICA

VAN REES PRESS • NEW YORK

# *Preface*

THIS TEXT IS planned for use in orientation courses for freshman women majoring in physical education, health education, and recreation. Most of these orientation courses are given separately to men and women, but few of the texts give attention to content of special interest to women students. For this reason the author decided to write the text primarily for women. However, it will be a useful reference in men's orientation classes and in co-educational courses in methods and principles at the junior and senior level. In addition it will be a resource for high-school girls who are considering this field as a career.

In teaching our first orientation course the author found that freshmen wanted to know what they would be doing day by day on the job. They needed to get an idea of what they might accomplish over a longer time, and this helped them to understand the reason for various courses in their own curriculum. Guidance in working toward their goals and in evaluating their progress, as well as a broad view of the many opportunities and responsibilities ahead of them, were other outcomes of the course.

Experience in advising upper-class students and surveying

alumnae opinion brought out the students' need both to prepare for homemaking as well as for a career and to plan this preparation as early as the freshman year. Chapter 3 discusses success in homemaking and college preparation for this role.

No professional student can understand the present status of his profession without knowing something about how it has developed. No young woman can appreciate her present-day opportunities without knowing how limited were the lives of earlier generations and how real the struggle against these limits. The historical chapters are designed to improve the freshman's understanding and appreciation of the early work of pioneers and of present-day attitudes toward health, physical education, and recreation. The last two chapters point up important problems still to be solved and contributions toward their solution that undergraduates as well as more experienced persons may make.

The author is grateful for all of the help received in preparing the text. The generous award of an Amy Morris Homans Fellowship from Wellesley College made much of the background study possible. The Washington office of the American Association for Health, Physical Education, and Recreation sent material from their files; many college departments gave information on orientation courses and curricular patterns and contributed illustrative material; school systems and college departments sent rating blanks; librarians, especially in the Library of Congress and in Mary Hemenway Hall, have gone well "beyond the line of duty" in hunting up material; freshman major students at the State University of Iowa, the University of Colorado, and Colorado State College at Greeley took time to read portions of the manuscript and to comment on vocabulary, readability, and usefulness of content; four teachers and a former recreation worker wrote descriptions of their work. All of this co-operation has proved indispensable. Among the many colleagues and other friends who have read all or parts of the manuscript and who have made very valu-

able suggestions, the author would like to thank Marie Ort-
mayer, Mildred Doster, Elizabeth Kelley, Dudley Ashton,
Dorothy Zirbes, Lois Broady, Henry Rowland Halsey, and
the always-helpful staff of G. P. Putnam's Sons.

Elizabeth Halsey

Littleton, Colorado, 1960

# Contents

# Women in Physical Education

# CHAPTER 1

# Important Work

IN THE UNITED STATES, on any schoolday morning, more than 34 million secondary-school children get in the car-pool car or on the school bus and go off to school. Or, in a different situation, they run or dawdle down the street and around the corner to their neighborhood school building. On the same morning about 10 million high-school youth rejoin their pals at school and take up again their more or less clear trails to the future. Meanwhile nearly 4 million of their older brothers and sisters in college are getting themselves to the first class of their campus day. This is a very large number of small and large people for this country to educate. In fact it is more than a fourth of our total population.

## Children and youth in school determine the country's future

However large the task of education, it must not be done in a careless way. Poor procedure in our educational program cannot be allowed when so many lives are involved, so much money is being spent, and so much of our country's future is at stake. Somewhere in that great number of children and

youth is the boy or girl who will be the President of the
United States and his first lady some thirty to fifty years from
this day. There also are our future senators, cabinet members,
judges, inventors, teachers, clergymen, ambassadors, busi-
nessmen, farmers, ranchers, skilled and unskilled workers,
and all the other men and women who will carry on the
jobs your parents are doing now. These youngsters, in turn,
will also be parents, home makers, and voters. How good will
they be at the jobs they have ahead of them? How good will
their lives be?

The answers to these questions depend on what they are
learning at home, in school, church, or community groups,
and what they are learning from each other. All of this learning is, of course, conditioned by the gifts of ability they have
at birth. What they are learning in school is the result of a carefully planned program, entrusted to more than a million
and a half teachers, supervisors, and administrators. What
they are learning in community centers is also planned and
supervised.

Three important parts of school and community programs
are closely related: physical education, health education, and
recreation. This book is written to describe these fields, and
the work of women teachers and leaders who have chosen
these fields for their careers. It should help to orient students
who are beginning their preparation.

## Health, physical education, and recreation compared

Physical education has recently been defined as "the use
of vigorous activity as planned developmental experience."
This definition goes well beyond the popular idea of calisthenics, or varsity athletics, or just games. It implies a variety
of activities, carefully selected to fit the child's age and stage
of growth. These activities should be so taught that the total
experience is good. Usually school administrators plan phys-

ical education as a part of every child's day. Why? Because no child can develop as he should without active play, and no President, scientist, worker, or parent can do his best without the finest body he can build and maintain through vigorous activity. But neither play nor exercise of itself can make a fine body a part of a fine personality. In physical education, for instance, many experiences that accompany play help the child learn to control his temper, help the youth respect his opponent in a game, help the shy boy or girl work and play happily with others, and give all students opportunity to think out strategy and invent activities. Good teachers of physical education will find the way to teach all of these things directly or indirectly. That is why the work they do, day by day, is so important.

In simplest terms, health education is that part of the school procedure designed to promote the child's well-being. The healthy child is free from disease. More than that, he is in a state of complete physical, mental, and social well-being. The school usually attempts to protect the child through health services, to inform him through health instruction, and to surround him with a clean, safe, well-ventilated and generally healthful school environment. This is a broad responsibility, shared in part by all school personnel.

Recreation is what a person chooses to do because he finds the activity enjoyable. Too much emphasis on the end product rather than on the process is likely to destroy the relaxed "fun" nature of recreation. Community recreation programs select a variety of constructive and developmental activities for persons of all ages, in all seasons of the year, outdoors and indoors.

We say that every child in school should have the opportunity to develop fully his capacity for thinking, feeling, and doing at his own best level. Is this the goal of education? Yes, if we define the child's "best level" as best for others as well as himself. We should see him not only as one small person growing up, but as part of his family at home, his class at school, his group on the playground. In these groups he is learning to adjust, to understand his environment, increasingly broad in time and space, and his own increasing responsibility to improve that environment. To repeat: development of the individual to the best possible level for himself and for society is the ultimate goal of education. Thus it becomes the focus of all that we do in health, physical education, and recreation.

If health, physical education, and recreation have the same ultimate goal as education, how can future teachers and leaders in these fields distinguish their own fields? How can they think about the next steps or come "down to earth" and see what they can accomplish day by day? Each of these fields has its own way of working, which is different from the rest of the school procedures, and which has its own specific objectives.

Physical education uses vigorous activity on the school playground or in the gymnasium as experience planned to promote the child's favorable development. Health education uses classroom teaching, field experiences, and a number of such informal situations as selecting food in the lunchroom, morning health inspection, medical examinations, and health counseling as developmental experiences. Recreation uses a great variety of wholesome, constructive activities that will attract the child in his free time after school and on weekends.

Physical education's more specific objectives include: (1) physical development and fitness through a large amount of exercise; (2) skills of movement that will increase the student's competence, sense of security, and safety; (3) democratic social adjustment to others in his activity groups; (4) emotional control necessary to fair play and sportsman-like behavior—at his own level; (5) enjoyment of free movement, rhythmic movement, and games; (6) inventive exploration of movement and ways of improving movement skills. Health education has such specific objectives as: (1) improving the child's knowledge and interest in conduct leading to better health and safety for himself and others; (2) counseling and motivating children and parents for the correction of health defects; (3) preventing the spread of infectious disease; (4) maintaining a school environment that promotes both physical and mental health; (5) adapting school and home situations to meet the health needs of exceptional children; (6) co-ordinating school, home, and community efforts to improve health and safety.

Recreation also sets such definite objectives as: (1) developing recreational skills that give enjoyment, satisfaction, and some feeling of success; (2) providing for release of tensions; (3) exploring new experiences that yield new learnings and greater breadth of understanding; (4) improvement of social adjustment; (5) creative achievement; (6) community service; (7) strengthening of ethical codes.

It is obvious that any one of these careers is broad in outlook and important in service to children, adolescents, adults, and to society.

## Who are the men and women in this work?

To do this important work for more than forty-eight million children and youth, thousands of teachers and leaders are needed. Most of them are college graduates, and the most competent have had special training for their positions. Nearly half of them are men, most of whom teach and coach in high schools and colleges or Y.M.C.A.'s and recreation centers. Women usually teach in elementary schools, high schools, and colleges. Some of these teachers and leaders do other things also: they work with the physically handicapped in special schools or in hospitals, either as physical therapists or recreation therapists; they work with national health agencies, government agencies, voluntary youth groups, and commercial recreation projects or enterprises.

Why have they chosen these fields? Many of the physical education teachers say it is because they like activities such as sports, dance, stunts, and tumbling. Others say they like children, or that they want to work with teenagers, and some think it would be stimulating to live and work in a college world. A few have always planned to teach; others say they would like to teach but are afraid of behavior problems and have selected recreation, health, or physical education because they think that in these fields they might have better rapport with their groups and so could help them more readily. Those who work in health have interests in biological sciences, and many take nurses' training, physical therapy, or go on to medical degrees. All of this group are impressed with the fundamental importance of improving the health of our present and future citizens. Recreation leaders often say that they wish to work with young and old on a voluntary basis, that is, in activities the group likes and wants to do.

Some of the men have gone into the field through their interest in interscholastic athletics. If they have made a name for themselves as players on their high-school teams, they think, very naturally, of coaching as a career. Often they prepare for coaching and teaching physical education together, since most men work in both areas if they start in high-school positions. Coaching is such a large part of these combined jobs that orientation to coaching must be a large part of any introductory courses for men. However, it is beyond the scope of this book, which discusses woman's role in health, physical education, recreation, and successful homemaking. It is important for young men and young women in these fields to understand each other's problems: why some of their activities, policies, and curricular emphases differ; which courses and classes may profitably be co-educational; and how all of their work relates to the same background of science, general education, and professional education. Most schools develop these understandings in co-educational courses in methods and principles in the junior and senior years of the college professional course. Some of the historical reasons for the development of these differences will be apparent to the reader in later chapters.

## Specific situations: a look from the outside

This would be a good time for readers of the text to arrange with their instructor to visit some of the work we have been discussing. First, some verbal visits to hypothetical situations.

Here is one of Suburbia's finest new elementary schools. Not a bit like the traditional four-room, red brick box in the middle of a dusty playground, this colorful, glass-walled structure fronts on a wide lawn with handsome plantings. At the back is an all weather playground where the fourth grade is now coming outdoors for physical education. In groups the children are carrying mats, a long stout pole, and boxes of balls and small equipment. Quickly they take their places, put the mats on the ground near their apparatus, get balls out of one box, jump-ropes out of another, and are soon at play in their own groups. The group leaders help to see that everyone gets his turn or gets something to work with. The teacher, who has come out with the last group, seems to be everywhere. She answers questions about ball handling in one group, suggests a better way to hold on to the rings in another, encourages a boy who is having trouble with rhythm in jumping rope, and helps to adjust the mat at the horizontal ladder. Then she strikes a tom tom for attention, and asks three children at the ladder to show the others how to land lightly as they jump down. "What did you like about that?," she asks. The children have several comments, and she is interested in all of them, but brings out for emphasis "being easy, reaching down for the ground with their toes, then relaxing as soon as they land, even touching the mat with their hands as they bend their knees." After another two or three minutes the teacher signals for a change. Apparently they have agreed on a system of rotation, so they move on to the next station eagerly and start work without confusion. When we talk with the young teacher after class we comment on the fact that the children are all busy, and all seem to be interested in learning as they try different things. "Don't any of them have to be urged to participate or pushed to try their best?," we ask. "At first some did not want to try things," she said, "and we still have one or two who are not easy on any climbing apparatus. But we tried *not* pushing them. We let them see what fun the others are having, and then encouraged them to try simple things they thought they could do. It surprised me to see that they know rather well what they can do, and almost never get into situations that are dangerous for them. This plan worked, because very soon they were all doing most of the things anyone is doing, and they invent new stunts and what they call 'tricks.' I never have to use rivalry to get them to do their best. Just a good word now and then for good work, and having the children evaluate what is going on is very stimulating. . . . That's what I like about this teaching: every child is different, and every child can be happy here while he's learning new skills, learning to work with his squad, and at the same time building a stronger body through all the exercise he gets."

We then go into the cheerful and orderly office of the school nurse, who has just arranged to have the mother of a child showing symptoms of measles come to take him home. While waiting she shows us charts giving results of continuous medical supervision through repeated medical examinations and also safety posters made by the sixth grade in art. In addition to making safety posters, she explains, the sixth grade has a safety committee that inspects school grounds each day for such hazards as tin cans or broken glass on the playground. Along one wall are attractive nutrition exhibits illustrating balanced menus, and there is posted a list of school lunch menus for the month. We learn that these are sent home with the children and published weekly in the local papers so mothers may consider them in planning home meals. The nurse describes to us the co-operative effort of school board, school physician and nurses, superintendent and elementary-school principals in planning with the architect the health features of the new elementary-school buildings. Similar teamwork aids the room teacher in planning material for health instruction. She goes on to tell us about one of the interesting experiments tried by a fourth-grade teacher who worked out with her class an "Ask the Doctor" program toward the end of the year. It was so successful that the children wanted a similar "Ask the Dentist" program, but there was no school dentist available. "You can imagine the complications," said the young woman. "Every child wanted his favorite dentist, and since there are at least half a dozen in town, we had a real problem on our hands. That year they settled it by drawing lots, but it actually hastened the move the school board had been considering—appointment of a school dentist." The nurse goes on to say that her contacts with the homes are very challenging. It takes time to investigate defects with home visits, but she thinks the results in better understanding of the child's problems on her part, and greater interest in the work of the school on the part of the mother, are very well worth the time and effort. Occasionally she has arranged telephone conferences with a group of mothers when some immediate health problem could best be handled that way. The local telephone company has co-operated by calling a number of homes and holding the wire communication open during the discussion.[1] "This has been a great time saver," and then the nurse concluded our visit by summing up results: "It's interesting to see our program grow, and to check results in improved daily attendance records. Of course we hope there are long-time results also. We know the children are interested, and they are developing a friendly attitude toward this office as well as the

---

[1] Viola Grandstrom, "Health Education by Telephone," *Journal of School Health,* 29 (January 1959), 31.

doctor and dentist. We hear that this carries over to their own doctors and dentists."

This is almost an ideal situation, so we might go on to another, less favorable one. We look in at a high-school girls' class in a different town. They are in a small, rather dirty gymnasium. Neither the teachers nor the girls show any sign of interest as they go through some calisthenics in a listless fashion. Afterwards the teacher tells us that she majored in foreign language, but was asked to teach physical education at the last minute. "Really, I didn't know what to do with my classes, so I got an old book out of the library—it had some drills in it, which we have learned. They are pretty boring, but we do have fun playing basketball and volleyball after school. The girls are after me to sponsor a G.A.A., but I don't know how to go about getting it started." Later, in the superintendent's office, we ask about school health services and the community recreation program; we are told that they do not exist. "About ten years ago," said the superintendent, "the Rotary club raised some money for a playground, and they ran one on the school grounds for two summers. Then their money ran out and they became interested in something else."

Next we go back to the city, and visit the Y.W.C.A. A posture class for business girls practices moving easily as an office receptionist should, then various ways of sitting in a typewriter chair, next a brisk run-through of exercises to keep waists and hips in trim, and finally a quarter hour of volleyball. Down in the pool there is another class: high-school girls who are beginning swimmers and have just passed the first stages of balancing, moving, floating, and breathing. Teachers of both classes are easy, competent, and share the enthusiasm of their class members.

A look in at the city's school for exceptional children shows another possibility for the physical education and health teachers who take additional training. In the sunlight outdoors are half a dozen spastic children cheerfully matching their limited powers against obstacles. Three are trying to climb on a ladder that forms a low arc leading up, over, and down. Two are kicking a ball back and forth to each other. Another is riding a small bicycle in a fixed frame, which does not move or tip. Two teachers help, encourage, suggest, and guide them with close attention. This school also has a swimming pool, necessary for postpolio treatment. Here one child at a time tries those forms of swimming and water stunts that will gradually strengthen and re-educate damaged muscles. The teacher uses her own knowledge of muscle action as well as her experience in teaching swimming. If we had time we could go to the hospital and see other physical therapists at work, carrying out physicians' orders for massage, diathermy, adaptive exercise, and other prescribed treatment. We could also visit the recreation therapy department, in which games, crafts, and various hobbies are adapted to the patients' needs.

### Against Great Odds

This has been a brief look at some of the things graduates in health, physical education, and recreation are doing. There are many more. Our national professional association suggests in its name the breadth of its interests and the inclusive nature of its organization: the American Association for Health, Physical Education, and Recreation, usually abbreviated AAHPER. While most of its members are in physical education, there are many from all three fields—more than 22,000 in all. The same college course does not prepare for all of these related fields, as we shall see in Chapter 4. However, in the first two years of the undergraduate major, basic training for the three fields is somewhat similar. In the types of positions listed below there are several for which additional graduate specialization is considered necessary. These are marked with an asterisk *.

> Teaching physical education in the elementary school.
> Teaching physical education and coaching in the high school.
> Teaching physical education and coaching in the college.*
> Leading recreation in Y.M.C.A.'s, Y.W.C.A.'s, and community centers.
> Counseling in summer camps.
> Leading summer playground activities.
> Teaching health education, and work with health agencies.
> Practicing physical therapy in hospitals, offices, and clinics.*
> Practicing recreation therapy in hospitals and clinics.*
> Administering or supervising the work of others.*

Although there are thousands of persons in such positions, not nearly enough are adequately prepared for their work. Remember the high school where no one got much out of the lesson because the teacher had no training? Don't think that is an unusual situation. In small high schools where there are only two or three teachers, the chances are that none of them will be well qualified in health or physical education. In 80 per cent of our elementary schools physical education is taught by the classroom teacher. With help from the supervising specialist in physical education many of them do an excellent job, because they know the children so well. However, 60 per cent of them have no advice from a supervisor as to what activities to teach or how to teach them. It is estimated that we need at least three times as many qualified women physical education teachers as we now have if we are to give our children the instruction and guidance they need in this all-important field. That is why every competent, well-trained graduate now has her choice of many positions. The same situation exists in health education, physical therapy, and recreation leadership.

### Specific situations: accounts from the inside

It is valuable to visit different classes if we want to know what women in these fields are doing. One visit, however, shows only what is happening on one day. The worker herself can tell us what happens from day to day, and what makes up the different parts of her work. Only the person on the job can tell us whether she earns enough to live on and lives happily while she is earning; whether she finds the work satisfying; what her school is like; and what her town is like.

Several teachers and one recreation leader have done just this. They have written analyses of their work, and have given me permission to reprint their descriptions here, changing their names, and the names of their schools. In other words, the names of the writers and the names of their schools are fictitious. Everything else in each account is factual, as it has been set down by the person on the job.

### Susan Blake teaches in an elementary school in a Western city

The alarm rings at 7:15 A.M., and I hop out of bed and get ready for school. After breakfast I leave for school around

8:00 o'clock. Since my school is five miles from where I live, I leave in plenty of time. All regular session teachers are required to be in their rooms at 8:40. I arrive at school about 8:20 in time to enjoy a cup of coffee with other members of the faculty in the teachers' lounge. At 8:40 I go to my office and review my plans for the day. At 9:00 o'clock sharp the thirty-four eager and smiling children in my first grade enter the gym and sit down in their four rows, line leaders in front. Today we have rhythms, and I shall introduce some new singing games: the first is "Did You Ever See a Lassie?" To make it a little more meaningful, some history of the dances and singing games we perform comes first, so I ask if any one can tell me what a lassie is. One little boy shoots his hand in the air and replies: "It's a dog, and I watch him every Thursday night on T.V." Muffling a laugh I tell him he is absolutely right, and that the word "lassie" has another meaning also, which is then revealed to the class. So many things happen with young children, that each day brings an enlightening surprise.

My next two classes are another first grade, and a second grade. Each period is thirty minutes long. The fourth period is free, and I go to the teachers' lounge and visit with other teachers who have the same free period. Then I usually meet my fourth grade coming down the hall on their way to gym. They are quite a lively group, and ask me a million questions ranging from "What are we going to do today?" to "Are you a Democrat or a Republican"? The next thirty minutes is my planning period, and I usually meet with the other two physical education teachers for joint planning or select my own ideas to go over with them at a later time. At noon I go on playground duty for thirty-five minutes, and often get involved in a game of Four Square or Tether Ball. When I'm not playing I get told all about the new baby brother or sister who was just brought home from the hospital, or the new pair of roller skates, or the week end trip to the mountains. There are innumerable questions: "What time is it?" "May I have a jump rope?" "What is your first name?" "Did you see Howdy Doody on T.V. last night?" "Do you want to join our Elvis Presley club?" Often there are a few tears to dry as a result of skinned knees or bumped heads. Their boundless energy keeps me jumping, but I love it.

I eat my lunch at 12:35, and then four of us usually have a hand or two of bridge, before my next class—another first grade at 1:10. What fun they have in gym, as they call it! It's funny, but the motivation problem in physical education is practically nil. The children enjoy it so much that it makes teaching very easy. My next two classes are third grades, and what a difference between the two! The first one is extremely skilled; they become bored with third grade games, and it is a real challenge to keep up with them. The other third grade is extremely unskilled, and still love first and second grade games and activities. I feel that it is a definite advantage to have two classes of the same grade, to see what great differences there can be between children of the same school age. My last class of the day is an extremely energetic group of second graders, and nothing is too hard for them—they will try anything and everything. At 3:15 I go to the auditorium to meet all the children who ride buses. Upon their suggestion I have been reading to them the book of their choice. They are a very good audience, and many times I have to shoo them out of the building if the bus comes when we are in a very exciting part of the book. When the last person is gone, and all is quiet in the hall, I meet my roommate and leave school; around 3:30. So ends a typical day of school.

There are additional duties on other days. I am in charge of the children's safety patrol at my school. We have a meeting once a week, and also we have a safety court which meets once a week during the noon hour. The court consists of the captain and lieutenant of the safety patrol, and several of its outstanding members. Habitual offenders are brought before the court, their cases are reviewed, and the penalties are given and enforced.

We also have a teachers' meeting once a week, and P.T.A. meetings once a month.

Occasionally I have been asked to accompany different classes on field trips, which is lots of fun. I went with the fourth grade to visit and tour a railroad terminal. I also chaperoned the fifth and sixth grades to hear the city's Symphony Orchestra.

Where does my money go? Here are the percentages figured on the amount I get each of twelve months, after deductions.

|  |  |  |
|---:|:---|:---|
| 10.4 | % | Food |
| 16.6 | % | Housing |
| 16.6 | % | Clothing and personal care |
| 4.2 | % | Contributions |
| 10.4 | % | Recreation and transportation |
| 8.3 | % | Savings and insurance |
| 12.5 | % | Spending money |
| 4.2 | % | Gifts |
| 16.8 | % | Miscellaneous |
| 100.00 | % | Total |

For recreation, sightseeing has been one of my chief interests since arriving in this state. I have taken several trips to the National Parks and cities near by. I have also taken up skiing, and took my first lesson in one of the mountain ski resorts. What fun I had!

Teachers in our school have organized a bridge club, which meets once a month at the various members' homes.

One weekend four of us went camping in the mountains. We took sleeping bags and our camping equipment, and really had a good time. It was in the early fall, and the scenery was lovely with the red, rust, orange, and yellow leaves of the turning aspen.

We have become very enthusiastic about ice hockey, which

is a new game to us. We have seen several games now, and think it is great. Donning our long red woolies we go ice skating in one of the parks. Such an invigorating sport—something we haven't enjoyed since we were kids. Of course movies, bowling, and riding remain as old time favorites.

I have thoroughly enjoyed my community as a place to work and live. It has been entirely what I expected, and more. I am very pleased with my selection for my first year of teaching. I have met so many wonderful people, and have learned a great deal in this short time, not only in teaching, but in being on my own for the first time in my life. Budgeting money and sharing in the general management of an apartment have been quite an experience.

My instructors in college told me that I would learn more during my first year of teaching than at any other time. Truer words were never spoken! I've learned so many little things which are not found in books. There are some headaches, which are to be expected, and I'm sure you will find them in any type of work. I feel that the satisfaction I have gained through teaching physical education completely overshadows the headaches. If I were to list all the satisfactions it would take volumes. I have found so many little things gratifying: the beaming smile of a little boy who finally after hours of practice learns to punt a soccer ball; a little first grade girl who can't skip—I work and work each day with her, but never seem to make any progress—then one Monday morning she comes to class so excited she can hardly talk—yes, she has learned to skip. She thanks me over and over for helping her. Although she conquered it on her own, she still gives me all the credit. It is the little things like this which nearly bring tears to my eyes.

As far as my future is concerned I can't say. Although I am going to be married next summer, I still plan to continue teaching. Since my fiance's work will require us to live in a college town, I hope to take graduate work and eventually get my Master's degree.

### *Dorothy Hale McDowell is in an Eastern suburban Junior High School*

Following my graduation from college, I realize that I had obtained two very important keys to my future. First, I had received four enjoyable years of academic and social growth; and second, I had become confident that my training would result in a career that would be of both personal and community value. Today, after having taught for two years, I have come to understand more completely just how valuable my four years of college teacher training has been.

I teach physical education and general science at Collins Junior High School in Westford, Connecticut, and live with my husband in another Hartford suburb, Newtown. My husband commutes from our four and one-half room apartment to Hartford, where he is employed by an insurance firm. Our working day begins at the same time in the morning, and my day very conveniently ends a half hour before his, giving me some time to assume the role of housekeeper before he returns home.

Collins Junior High is one of the many fine schools found in Westford, and has an enrollment of 650 students. My position calls for the teaching of 8th grade general science eight periods per week and ten periods of physical education instruction in the 7th and 9th grades. My associate girls' physical education instructor teaches four periods of social studies and twelve physical education classes per week. Our school administrators feel that two instructors with class room subject responsibilities make the school day more balanced, enjoyable, and profitable for both the teacher and student. This same policy applies also to the two men who handle the boys' physical education program.

The enthusiasm of the girls for sports reflects the policies and theories of the school administration toward physical education. In addition to the two regular periods of physical education per week, *all* girls participate in the school intramural program. Each grade competes separately on teams formed in the individual home rooms, once a week during the last or sixth period of the day. This period is scheduled three days per week for intramurals, and two days per week for other club activities. After school sports also give the girls an additional period to participate in a sports program on an elective basis. As in the plan for intramurals, each of three grades has its special day each week for after school practice. Thus each week every girl has a minimum of three hours of sports activity with an opportunity for a fourth elective hour, plus two class periods of physical education.

A typical working day for me is busy but balanced. It would include two hours of physical education classes, a free period, two hours of science instruction, lunch, intramurals, and then after school practice. On the two days per week when there are no intramurals, my sixth period may be spent correcting class work, counselling students, or perhaps helping the chorus director decide whether or not the alto section is too loud in one of the songs the chorus is preparing for a concert. In return, she is givig me piano lessons twice a week. It is truly amazing what a faculty accomplish when all quite freely give of their talents and resources.

The warmth of sincere friendliness and understanding that exists between the students, teachers, and parents, academically and socially, more than compensates for the few seemingly less enjoyable situations in which I find myself during the day. For example, a physical education person frequently becomes the nurse in the event of any emergency during the nurse's absence; during a free period it is not too uncommon to take over a Latin or algebra class if the regular teacher is called off unexpectedly on business for that period; there are faculty meetings one afternoon per month and physical education department meetings one afternoon per month; each year the state holds a Science Fair, and each eighth grader at Collins is required to design and build an entry under the guidance of his science instructor; and finally there are the P.T.A. meetings every other month which, although extremely beneficial both to parent and teacher, are still somewhat disturbing since they consume evening time after a full day has been spent at school. All in all it is only fair to say that many of these experiences often prove to be quite interesting and fun, while a few of them must just be considered a part of the job that you are there to do.

The most important part of my career, in addition to its opportunity for personal satisfaction and growth, is that it must provide financial security. If a woman is single, there must be ample salary to cover living expenses and offer savings possibilities for future retirement plans. Although there is not such an immediate need for good salary for the married woman who shares a husband's income in addition to her own, there is another aspect that is extremely important both to the woman teacher and to her husband. That is the security in knowing that she can be an additional or full time provider of income in every situation that may arise. This security is also somewhat comforting for a husband, since he knows his family would be adequately provided for in the event that his primary income for any reason should be lost.

In our part of the state women in business, on the average, receive far less financial compensation than do women in the teaching profession. Women in the teaching profession start at higher salaries and receive greater and more frequent salary increments than their business counterparts. Thus, in this area, I feel that a teacher has the advantage both of a respected professional position in the community, and of a very rewarding salary.

My husband and I have many plans for the future, all of which center about a home and a family. Our living expenses, which include renting an apartment, owning a car, food and recreation, are budgeted to fit into my husband's salary as much as is possible; and my income is set aside for the down payment on the home that we are planning to build. We are able to enjoy concerts, plays, occasional budget trips to New York for sight-seeing and shopping, and various sports. My husband and I share hobbies such as piano lessons, collecting records for our Hi-Fi set, and building all sorts of useful items included in do-it-yourself form. Oil painting lessons manage to fill out any other spare moments that I might have.

It is with a great deal of satisfaction that I realize that in a year or so our dream of a home and family will become a reality; also that I will be able to think of my teaching career as having been a part of the happiness of our past and the security of our future.

### *Joan Darby teaches in a small, well-established Liberal Arts College in the Midwest*

Each day, Monday through Friday, begins with my arrival at the gymnasium anywhere from 8:00 A.M. to 8:15 A.M. depending upon any preparation that should be made before the 8:45 class—and also, of course, on how quickly the coffee percolated that particular morning. Upon arrival at the office we are usually confronted with minor problems such as students who, after six months, have suddenly forgotten their locker combinations. When trial and error does not free the tenacious locks, they appear en masse, moments before class is scheduled to begin.

Although office hours run roughly from 8:15 to 12:00 in the morning, and from 1:15 to about 5:00 in the afternoon, only about three or four hours in the day are actually taken up with the teaching of classes. The remaining time is given to lesson preparation, counseling students, advising extra curricular departmental clubs, and such routine office work as reports, etc.

The classes taught in our department vary with the seasons. The fall term usually finds me either on the hockey field or teaching volleyball outdoors. The first winter term is spent in teaching some phase of tumbling and trampoline. The swimming pool is my warm hide-out when the snow blows and sub-zero temperatures prevail, during the second winter term. During the spring term I teach softball and archery out of doors, and return to the subterranean levels of the pool to teach advanced swimming.

Somehow night activities pop up quite often. For two weeks each school year we teach Red Cross Life Saving classes in the evenings, thus avoiding scheduling difficulties for a large number of students. Also, our intramural games are usually played in the evenings. In addition, the second semester brings our annual aquatic show, which seems to necessitate an endless number of evening practices. But when we view with pride the finished product, students and sponsor alike agree that all of the time and effort were well spent.

The "at home" hours, which at times seem rather few, are spent in a third story apartment. Three of us live on the third floor, sharing our ups and downs of the day, as well as our culinary triumphs and failures. Roughly, 35% of my income is spent on food, housing, and clothing; 10% on education and contributions; 15% on recreation, car, vacation trips; 15% on miscellaneous and insurance. The remaining 25% is put into savings. I find that it is always possible to save at least 25% of my income, and some months considerably more. This saving isn't the result of any particular restriction, but rather of having certain standards of living, and as your salary rises, sticking pretty much to your normal pattern; hence the saving. Also my annual income is increased by the salary I earn as counselor in summer camps. I often take such a position not necessarily because my school year income isn't sufficient, but because I thoroughly enjoy this type of work in the summer.

Leisure hours are usually spent with a good book or in listening to music. And when a free summer rolls around I enjoy puttering in a garden. By virtue of all the time and attention she requires, I consider my dog a hobby. Four of us adopted this homeless pet a year ago, and we share the walking duties in sub-zero weather.

In these tense and nervous times we hear a lot about freedom of teaching. They say that when you have this freedom you don't appreciate it. To this adage I consider myself an exception, however. Our college prides itself on freedom of teaching and freedom of thought. It isn't that we have theories that could be questioned, but rather that it gives you security to know that you are free within the framework of freedom.

Our community is rather small. It is peculiar in that it is primarily a residential community rather than a mixture of business district and homes. Downtown consists of a movie, a cafe, one drug store, a variety store, two clothing stores, and two hardware stores and several other small businesses. A large proportion of the people living in the community are employed in a nearby city twelve miles away. We have the opportunity of living in a small town with all of its advantages, yet have also the advantages of a city which is but a fifteen minute drive.

Our town is a very friendly place. The townspeople are interested in the college and all of its many activities. In turn they welcome us into all of their various clubs and organizations. My greatest contact with the community has come through my active participation in the League of Women Voters. This has given me the opportunity to learn of the problems and progress of the city government, and an opportunity to become well acquainted with women and men of the community. By and large, our community gives me very nicely the type of life which I enjoy: friendly interesting people, a quiet life away from the stress and strains of the city, yet with the advantage of the city within a few minutes' drive.

In a fair and final evaluation of my job, it is an understatement to say that I am pleased. We have ups and downs, just as any people have in any jobs; without ups and downs we'll have to admit that life would be boring. I feel very fortunate to have chosen physical education as my major in college. It offers a challenging field of teaching, and its teaching is a constant source of fun and pleasure to me.

One of the things that is hard to express without experiencing it is your associations in a small college like this. It is pretty nice to forget your problems once or twice a day, drop a dime in your pocket, walk over the crest of the hill and down to the student union. There amid milling students and a blaring juke box you can usually find three or four faculty members huddled over steaming cups of coffee discussing politics, the Wednesday night fights, Picasso, the mechanical construction of an outer space satellite, or something comparable. You may not know much about any of these things, but if you sip your coffee slowly and listen, you are surprised at how much you learn, and how interesting things and people are.

### Hilda Nelson Brown was director of a recreation center in a Western city

After graduating with a major in recreation from the University, I was fortunate in securing a position in a good community recreation system. This was well coordinated with the school system so that many schools were used as recreation centers also. After my marriage I continued my work, and even after my first baby came it was possible to arrange that from the time I left home until my husband returned he could be left with a neighbor who had excellent training and ability in child care. But when he grew older, and before the second baby came I resigned in order to give all my time to the family. When my children are grown I hope to go back to recreation work at least part time. This account is written after three years away from the job.

My position was classified as Recreation Center Director II. The center assigned to me was located in an elementary school building in a middle income residential area. Using school facilities for public recreation is governed by a City-School Co-ordinating Committee, which has equal representation from the city and from the schools. A list of a center director's duties would include:

1) Develops and directs a recreational program in accordance with the needs and interests of the community
2) Confers with city-wide and community groups in determining a program for special groups
3) Organizes, directs, and supervises a variety of recreational activities
4) Supervises students who participate in the recreation program as a part of their training curriculum
5) Keeps records of the use of facilities and attendance; prepares monthly reports
6) Performs related work as required

It is important to note how a recreation center operates within a school building. The gymnasium and auditorium were reserved for our use during the after school hours when our program was in session. We used our own equipment and kept it stored in our small office off the gymnasium. Even though we were not school employees, we must maintain good working relationships with the school personnel, particularly the principal. I conferred with our principal regularly and endeavored to keep him fully informed about our activities. It was necessary to get his permission to use the school lunch room and the P.T.A. kitchen when we served refreshments. As long as our program was running smoothly with no damage to the school property the principal supported the center. The head custodian and night custodian were most critical toward the center activities. It was often necessary to remind them of our status. The best policy was to concentrate on the job, and maintain good discipline in our programs.

My center officially opened at 3:15 in the afternoon when the school children were dismissed. A typical Thursday would find me at the gymnasium door greeting 35 or 40 fifth and sixth grade pupils eagerly anticipating their weekly social hour, and displaying that after-school burst of energy. My staff worker and I would usually begin the session with an active party game. Their main interests in social activities were to learn basic dance steps and to have fun participating in mixers, musical games, or square dancing. The girls, typically aggressive at this age, would decide which boy they wanted for a partner and bodily pull him onto the floor. Surprisingly enough the boys did dance and even asked for certain records or requested favorite mixers. On special occasions, such as holidays, the group would choose a committee which would meet with us and plan a party.

All of our afternoon programs closed at 5:00, giving the custodian time to sweep the gymnasium floor before evening activities began. My staff worker and I would use this time for lunch and walk to a small shopping area a few blocks from school. The menu was limited but the people were friendly, and we always felt that we sacrificed good food for good public relations. A few parents or teen-agers would invariably drop in to chat with us or ask questions about the center program.

By 5:45 the teen-age boys were assembling at the back gymnasium door. This was their night to practice basketball and they wanted to be there for the full two hours. My staff worker had charge of all the boys' activities.

The modern dance group was due to arrive and I must take the record player with records onto the stage of the auditorium. This group consisted of approximately a dozen boys and girls, ages six to eight, and about six girls ages ten to twelve. The entire group met at 6:00 P.M. for warm-up, with a different child leading the exercises each time. Then the younger children would dance for a half hour. They enjoyed telling stories through creative movement, moving freely to record selections and composing simple group numbers. After the young ones left the older girls danced for forty-five minutes. Often they would plan a number to present at a scout meeting or Mother's club. My role was primarily to teach and demonstrate new exercises and coach their dancing. I injected music appreciation through my choice of records for background music. It was a real thrill to observe these uninhibited children perform their own creations.

Now it was time to greet the square dance caller and pianist. As I scurried back to the gymnasium I hoped the teen-age boys had left willingly when their practice session was over. In limited facilities the program runs more smoothly if the various interest groups are kept separate. The boys had gone, the caller was already setting up his public address system, and soon the gymnasium would be filled with the shouting and shuffling of gay square dancers. This was our most popular adult activity, drawing around one hundred dancers each Thursday night. The caller kept them on their toes all evening, pausing only to teach new steps or slow down the pace with a couple dance. During these two hours I assisted the caller with teaching, collected a small fee from each couple (to help cover the cost of the caller and pianist) and acted as hostess for the evening. It was a colorful sight watching the array of bright full skirts and cowboy shirts. At 10:00 the dance was over, and I locked up the equipment room for the night. The custodian was sweeping the floor, undoubtedly happy to see us leave.

As I drove home I mused over the events of the day: 10:00 A.M. had found me at the city administration building turning in time cards and attendance reports to our supervisor. From there I had accompanied other center directors to a luncheon meeting of the Area Welfare Council, Leisure Time Division, and heard a panel discuss "the Rise in Juvenile Delinquency." This meeting adjourned just in time for me to reach my center for the afternoon program.

In public recreation work I found that one is continually involved in an exchange of ideas. It is vitally important to keep abreast with latest developments in the field. Our center directors held a monthly meeting to present new ideas, discuss mutual problems, and plan city-wide events. We were governed by our elected officers with our immediate supervisor the only "outsider" who attended. Many worthwhile projects were accomplished through this exchange of ideas:

(1) Organized and directed inter-center basketball and softball leagues
(2) Planned and presented all-center stage productions
(3) Established a fund to send two representatives from our center directors to the National Recreation Convention
(4) Instituted a yearly spring workshop to formulate plans for summer program

There are both advantages and disadvantages in choosing recreation for a profession. The fact that your primary purpose is to help people have fun makes your job fun, too. You meet all types of people in every age group in a friendly atmosphere. I appreciated being out-of-doors supervising children almost the year round. Your efforts were rewarded daily by sincere thanks from children for helping them learn a new skill, or from parents who expressed their gratitude because you took an interest in their projects. You have freedom in planning your work that is not often possible in other jobs. In this way you can meet the needs of your particular neighborhood.

The biggest disadvantage in recreation is the abnormal working schedule. Since you are working with people in their leisure time you are on duty in the afternoons and evenings. Your hours on the job are also irregular—you are frequently required to attend meetings or conferences in the morning. Many times your day is broken up so your own leisure time may consist of an hour or two between a meeting and the time you are due at your center. I mixed a recreation career with marriage, but fortunately my understanding husband didn't mind eating dinner at 10:00 P.M. and had hobbies to keep him occupied during the evenings. Another undesirable feature of recreation centers is their location. Most centers are found in areas of greatest need—often old crowded sections of the city. Women directors, especially, are not anxious to cope with the problems these areas can create. However, any skilled director with a capable staff can handle difficult situations.

Like other employees we were free to pursue our own recreation on week-ends. Since both my husband and I prefer active outdoor sports, we have used the mountains to full advantage by skiing or hiking on the slopes, camping in the forests and boating on the streams. The children participate as much as they can, and even now are outdoor enthusiasts.

That there is a "career future" in each of these three professions is demonstrated by the numbers of women who are well-established and successful in them. Many are in administrative positions, and find a satisfaction in working out plans with their staff and seeing these plans carried out as obstacles are overcome. Some who have specialized enjoy the rewards of writing and research; others like the opportunities for counseling and guidance. As one administrator described student conferences: "The problems range from the seemingly trivial and unimportant to problems of great seriousness. Sometimes during these conferences there are tears, sometimes laughter, but always the problems are very real to those who bring them in. Often times I feel as if I must be a combination book of knowledge, judge, mother, priest, physician, and psychiatrist. Because I am not all these things, for the most part I simply listen." Several successful women have said that the human factor counts most: "All the fine speeches and honors are enjoyable, but not half as important as seeing our students change and grow while on the campus, and watching their development after graduation, either on the job or in their own homes." "Finally, the satisfactions gained from my job are many. Most of these are intangibles. The description of an average working day might not sound particularly interesting, but it is. It's exciting and stimulating because I am working with real people in real problems, and the opportunities I have for helping young people achieve success and a measure of happiness are important. It is a friendly kind of job. It is also homely and commonplace, yet there is always the possibility that when I least expect it I will experience one of those cherished 'high moments' in living. Constantly changing, constantly challenging, are descriptive terms for my job. To me people are the most important creatures on this earth. I like working closely with them."

## Advantages and disadvantages of teaching

Many of the advantages and disadvantages of teaching have come out in what the teachers say about their work. Perhaps it will be of help to the reader for me to summarize at this point.

1. Teaching is distinguished service. Do you remember Nathan Hale's statue? There was the poised, courageous young soldier, caught as a spy, whose regret was not that he was to lose his life, but that he had only one life to give to his country? Nathan Hale was also a teacher, and a teacher, says General Omar Bradley, has an advantage over the soldier in that he gives many lives to his country—the enriched lives of children who have been put in his care. Erasmus, the great Dutch teacher and writer said this in a striking way, many years ago:

> To be a schoolmaster is next to being a king. Do you count it a mean employment to embue the minds of your fellow citizens in their earnest years with the best literature and with the love of Christ, and to return them to their country honest and virtuous men? In the opinion of fools it is a humble task, but in fact it is the noblest of occupations.[2]

2. Teaching gives the satisfaction of a clear and unselfish purpose. The teacher looks at each child, each person of any

[2] Quoted by D. Louise Sharp, ed., *Why Teach* (New York: Henry Holt and Co., 1957), p. 4. By permission.

age as a human being who is growing and developing. The teacher's purpose is to understand and to help humans grow and develop desirably. He does not see people as consumers who may buy his goods if he understands how to appeal to them, as acquaintances who will do favors for him if he understands how to manipulate them, or as TV watchers who will turn off his show if he doesn't understand how to entertain them. In brief, he does not try to use people for *his own gain;* he tries to serve *their best development,* each as a person who has a right to favorable development.

3.  Fortunately, when the teacher looks at children or youth as persons, the third great advantage appears. Teaching becomes exciting fun. To see each of these small persons change, discover new things he can do, new facts he has found out, is to share the child's fascination with the world as the school shows it to him. Russell Crouse describes the progress of his children as follows:

> I saw him (the small son) make one discovery after another— each with a new sense of excitement. When I looked behind these almost-daily thrills, I found a teacher—a woman who looked upon her profession as something more than a day's work. . . . Fortunately his teachers have all been fellow adventurers. Now his sister has been drawn into this game. She has caught from him the eagerness, and from her teachers the enthusiasm. Now they both burst into the house at the end of a school day as though they had just climbed Mt. Everest.[3]

Then, too, children are highly amusing. They make funny faces, and as the best seller puts it, they "say the darnedest things." Some have a flair for planned comedy, some are most entertaining when they don't know it. The general testimony is that there is "never a dull moment" for the teacher with a sense of humor.

---

[3] Sharp, *op. cit.,* p. 40.

4. Teaching is fine preparation for parenthood, and vice versa. To study child development and to see it happen in the school is a good combination of theory and practice. Mothers who have been teachers are not as likely to be confused or perhaps frightened when their own children present problems. Then, too, the mother who has been a teacher, and who wants to go back to work after her children are grown, has a rich and broad background of experience which usually improves her teaching.

5. The teacher is respected by the community. Of course this relationship between teacher and community depends a great deal on the community, but even more on the temperament of the teacher. If the teacher enjoys people, is ready to take part in the organizations and projects found in most American cities and towns, it will not be long before he has a real share in those organizations. Most towns accept teachers as desirable members of the community, and acceptance (if returned) grows into liking and friendship.

6. The teacher is stimulated to develop as a person. His profession presents many rewards for study and investigation, and his summer "vacation" is long enough to make this possible. When he goes back to a college campus, in contact with other teachers in similar situations, he grows as he exchanges ideas, hears of new developments, and plans new solutions to familiar problems. Teaching need never be a blind alley.

Of course there are disadvantages in teaching as in every calling.

1. There is little opportunity to make a fortune from teaching, although it is almost always possible for the qualified teacher to make a better-than-average living. However, teachers' salaries are low in comparison with those of highly skilled labor and with successful members of such professions as law and medicine.

2. Teachers rarely become famous, although some famous

persons have been teachers.[4] If you have a vaulting ambition to become known from coast to coast, to see your name in the headlines, or to give such conspicuous service that you'll be highly rewarded by a grateful world, you had better look to another career.

3. Some schools demand so much "paper work," that is, reports and grades, and impose so many extracurricular duties on the teacher that he has little time left for his own recreation.

4. In some communities teachers feel that their recreation, their off-the-job living is closely watched and limited by critical supervision of the community "elders."

5. There are many schools so limited in equipment, in outlook, and in community support that the life of the teacher also seems limited. In the face of these obstacles, it takes courage and persistence to see the situation as a challenge, and to keep on working for better school living for the children.

## Advantages and disadvantages of teaching physical education

Are there advantages and disadvantages in teaching physical education different from those experienced by most other teachers? Of course those in physical education share the rewards and frustrations of all teachers. In addition there are others, perhaps unique to our field.

1. The enjoyment factor is greater. Children love activity, and have a great time moving freely in the play area. Teachers may share this gaiety of children as they play, even if they do not actually enter into the game. It is a fine reward to see faces in the schoolroom light up when it is time to go to the gymnasium. It is flattering to have children transfer their enjoy-

---

[4] Woodrow Wilson, Senator Paul Douglas, and Lillian Gilbreth are a few examples.

## "You do lively things with us"

ment of the class to liking for the teacher. As one small boy put it: "I like you because you do lively things with us."

2. The results of well-taught classes are very obvious. Schoolroom tensions from holding one position and using small muscles, schoolroom lethargy built up by "just sitting," vanish with laughter and large movement in space, with natural movement so necessary to the well-being of all humans. Skills develop rapidly, strength and endurance increase, children learn to get along together, to control their emotions, and to consider the feelings of other children. Sportsmanship, or the "Golden Rule of games" develops slowly, painfully at times, but very definitely over the months and years if the teacher knows how to guide the development.

3. Orderly procedure is much more readily developed in physical education classes than in others. It is easy to keep children too busy for mischief, easy to control poor conduct by pointing out how much time it takes away from play.

4. There is great opportunity for the teacher himself to develop in what is a comparatively new field. Much study and research are needed in physical education. Graduate programs have grown rapidly in the last quarter century. The enterprising

teacher finds much to challenge him: he needs better understanding of children, of movement, of competition, of total fitness, to mention just a few of the problems which interest us.[5]

5. The teacher may increase his own recreation resources
as he teaches. He improves his skills in individual sports and
such outdoor fun as skiing, riding, camping, fishing, and hunting. This may come about almost casually through participation in informal outing groups, or it may be the result of leading
scout troops or belonging to adult clubs.

On the other hand there are certain disadvantages.

1. The public doesn't understand modern physical education. Often school boards, administrators, teachers in other
fields, and even parents are likely to think of physical education
as it was in their day: calisthenics. Or they think of it as varsity
athletics, with all the problems inherent in that program. If a
young teacher lacks the stability and the sense of humor necessary to take friendly criticism or teasing without resentment, or
unfriendly criticism without retreat, these things may really
bother him. Yet if he knows that the present trend of science
and society is to emphasize all-around development, if he is
sure of his ground and has acceptable ways of developing the
prestige of his field, he may find this lack of understanding an
opportunity instead of an obstacle.

2. It is often said that teaching physical education is a
short-term career. Young men in coaching may find that a los-
ing season points toward a change of jobs. That is why it is a
good idea to be equipped to teach physical education, health,
and other subjects. Young women often think that youth and
youthful energy are essential for teaching activity courses. Of
course eight out of ten of them will marry within a few years
after graduation; and for those who do not there are excellent

---

[5] See Chap. 8 and 9 for a more complete discussion of these problems.

opportunities for promotion and the development of a satisfying career.

3.  The great attractiveness of sports, or of specialization in any one sport, may be a limiting factor for some coaches and teachers. If all his leisure is taken up by swimming or skiing, if all his reading is on the sport pages, and if TV has no attractions except sport events, he is living, unrealistically, in a small world. On the other hand, breadth of interest may easily be found on the campus—in general courses and a variety of extracurricular activities.

## Advantages and disadvantages of teaching health

Some of the advantages found in teaching health are as follows:

1.  The health education teacher or school nurse has immediate evidence that his work is important, since he can see the results of much of it. For instance, such health services as discovering and correcting defects in vision and hearing may change the child's entire outlook and school progress.

2.  Similarly important are the long-time results of an aroused interest in good health practices and habits.

3.  Health work is one of the best ways of bringing school and community agencies together and of helping parents to understand and co-operate with the school program.

4.  Informal contacts with children bring great teaching opportunities as well as rewards of human interest. Children respect the competent health education teacher and come to him for counseling; the follow-up work brings contacts with home conditions that make counseling more effective.

5.  In such a comparatively new field as this there is opportunity for the teacher to do creative work, to study, and to grow on the job.

6. There are many interesting positions in health work outside the school in such national agencies as the National Tuberculosis Association, the American Heart Association, the National Foundation for Infantile Paralysis, life insurance companies, and government agencies on the state and national level.

To some individuals the following facts may represent disadvantages:

1. Often the health education teacher or school nurse has only a vague assignment of his duties and responsibilities. His work may be as broad or as limited as his own qualifications, energy, and the superintendent's interest permit.

2. Responsibility for pupils' health is very serious; it may not always be possible to secure medical advice and help when needed.

3. It may be difficult to make the content of health teaching, which sounds familiar but is often remote from a child's natural interests, seem attractive or important to children.

4. Practically all health problems involve co-ordinated action for their prolonged treatment. To some the idea of arranging conferences and developing good working arrangements in a group, then continuing the slow process of discussing, planning, carrying out and evaluating plans, replanning after mistakes show up, seems a difficult process beyond the limits of patience.

5. The conscientious health teacher's work is never done. His telephone keeps him at the service of parents and pupils after hours, and for no overtime pay!

## Advantages and disadvantages of recreation leadership

Recreation makes a strong appeal to young people, for these (and perhaps many other) reasons:

1. The recreation leader helps people in the things they want to do, rather than in the things they have to do.

2. Therefore it is easy to establish pleasant relationships with them and to create an atmosphere of fun or satisfaction. This factor is especially appealing to the young person whose school experience has not included much fun or satisfaction.

3. The program is broad and varied, including sports, dance, dramatics, crafts, music, discussion and service clubs, and many other things people like to do.

4. The recreation leader works with all types of persons of different age levels and may have even better opportunities to help them than the teacher has. This is especially noteworthy in recreation therapy and in work with emotionally disturbed children.

5. In recreation the leader learns how to handle groups and to fit individuals into groups appropriate for them. He also works closely with individuals as a "practical psychologist."

6. Camp counselors find children in camp exposed to "teachable moments" throughout the day. Under the right influence they develop rapidly.

However, even in a camp situation all is not fun and play. Camp directors often complain that the counselors they hire have a fine vacation attitude, as far as their own summer's work goes. So with all recreation jobs it is important to look at the disadvantages.

1. The leader in a community recreation program has a schedule that makes his own recreation a rather solitary pursuit. His job begins when others are free from theirs. He is on duty in the evening, although he usually has time off in the morning when other people have gone to work. He may also have Sunday free.

2. Salaries in recreation positions tend to be lower than in teaching, and vacations are too short to permit summer study.

3.   As the most recent responsibility adopted by government, recreation departments and budgets are expanding, but they are also vulnerable to cuts in times of tax retrenchment.

4.   Since any recreation group fluctuates in attendance, planning is difficult and evaluation of progress almost impossible. This tends to produce some desirable and some undesirable qualities in the leader: spontaneity, enthusiasm, and flexibility on the one hand, but also superficiality and perhaps carelessness.

5.   In voluntary agencies such as Y.M.C.A.'s and Y.W.C.A.'s, money-raising is always a necessity. All of the personnel are expected to help with this work and considerable pressure is put on those in charge of dance and swimming, the two most lucrative activities. Not only must class attendance bring in a profit, but public programs also.

6.   In commercial recreation agencies the profit pressure on personnel is always there. This is especially true of new summer hotels, hotel camps, and children's camps, struggling to get established.[6]

7.   Many recreation jobs are blind alleys. Good administrators and supervisors are always in demand, but some activity specialists in skiing, swimming, dancing, and riding find the future diminishing instead of expanding in outlook.

Whatever your temperament, and however great your interest in these careers, it is important to review as realistically as you can their respective advantages and disadvantages—not only those discussed here but those you may hear of elsewhere. Talk them over with your advisers, your classmates, your parents, and best of all, with successful persons on the job. As you read the other chapters in the text look for more about these professions: find out what they demand in qualities and preparation; what

---

[6] An exceptionally vivid description of the work of a social director may be found in a recent autobiography, *Moss Hart: Act One* (New York: Random House, 1959), pp. 236–56.

they have contributed to American education; how they may develop in the future; and what they may mean to your future. Then your choice will be made intelligently, on a solid basis of fact.

## QUESTIONS

1. Do you agree with the statement that most children and youth in schools are scheduled for physical education? Was this true in your case? Do you think it is necessary? Why?

2. With the help of your instructor in planning and securing permission, visit some good work in elementary- and high-school physical education. Also in community recreation, health education, and physical therapy. Discuss what you saw in class.

3. Can you think of additional advantages or disadvantages of careers in the three fields? Which advantages or disadvantages seem most important to you?

4. Interview five of your friends who have already selected their careers, either in your major field or some other one. Find out what influenced them most in making their choice. Are there any factors that influenced all of them?

5. Which of the following terms best describes the work of young women in health, physical education or recreation?

|   |   |   |   |
|---|---|---|---|
| a. | Occupation | f. | Trade |
| b. | Vocation | g. | Skilled labor |
| c. | Avocation | h. | Service |
| d. | Profession | i. | Work |
| e. | Business | j. | Management |

6. Can you illustrate each of the other terms?

7. Are salaries in these fields high enough?

8. Are incomes in your home town as high as the income of the average woman in business?

9. From analyzing specific situations—either those you have seen or those described in the text—which objectives in your field are most readily attained? Which are most difficult? Are there some that belong to other fields also?

## SELECTED REFERENCES

*Physical Education for High School Students* (Washington, 1955), Chap. I and II.

Bucher, Charles. *Foundations of Physical Education,* 2nd ed. (St. Louis: Mosby, 1956), Chap. I–IV, VIII, IX, X.

Fitzgerald, Gerald. "Recreation as Your Career," *Journal AAHPER,* 23 (November 1952), 27.

Jenny, John H. *Introduction to Recreation Education* (Philadelphia: Saunders, 1955), Chap. II and Appendix A.

Knapp, Clyde and Ann E. Jewett. *Physical Education Student and Beginning Teacher* (New York: McGraw-Hill, 1957), Chap. I.

Sharp, D. Louise, ed. *Why Teach* (New York: Holt, 1957), pp. 21–31.

Smith, Julian. *Outdoor Education for American Youth* (Washington: AAHPER 1957), Chap. I.

Committee on Professional Preparation in Health Education of the American School Health Association, "Recommended Preparation for School Health Personnel," *U.S. Journal of School Health,* 27 (October and December 1957), 215–90.

# CHAPTER 2

# *Success in Work*

FOR THE IMPORTANT work of health, physical education, and recreation, it is very necessary that we know how to select good candidates, encourage those who will be successful, and prevent failures. Trying to predict success is always difficult, as personnel managers in large and small organizations have discovered despite many years of research. There are very few tests that will always be useful; none has as yet been found generally satisfactory in teaching or recreation leadership.

### Selection of candidates

Perhaps it is the scarcity of valid and reliable tests that has led most colleges to select candidates after they have been in college rather than when they enter college. However, obvious disabilities such as obesity, weak hearts, bone and joint defects, speech and hearing handicaps, and very low motor ability or mental ability scores will be considered by most advisers as sufficient reasons for nonadmission to professional courses. If social maladjustment appears on the applicant's record, this will be a deterrent to his teaching or recreation leadership. Later selection, during college training, gives both faculty and students an opportunity to estimate chances for a happy and satisfactory career in these fields.

## Qualities considered important for success

Both employers (school administrators) and advisers (faculty members of the departments concerned) have expressed opinions as to qualities they consider important for success. Rating blanks are used in teacher training institutions for guidance of students and by school administrators to evaluate applicants for positions; they are also used to rate teachers in service, both for improvement of teaching and for promotion. The opinions on three sets of rating blanks are summarized in Table I, with the percentage of the colleges and schools that mentioned each quality.

When studying the table, the reader should remember that rating blanks use very general terms, some of which are hard to define. Some terms seem to say the same thing as other terms, with a slightly different emphasis. When there are comparatively few colleges and cities reporting, the percentages do not have much statistical significance. Even with these limitations, however, it is interesting to note any similarities in the three lists. On what qualities do the employing schools and the teacher training colleges agree? Five things appear on each of the three lists: appearance, human relations, teaching skill, health, and professional attitude. Do the schools pick their teachers on one set of traits and promote them on another set? No, the traits on the application blank are repeated on the in-service blanks, except for personality and character, which are covered more specifically on the in-service blanks: friendly warmth, emotional stability, and public relations. There are other qualities rated when promotion is in question that depend on teachers' experience and adaptation to the school system: professional growth, understanding children, and interest in the

Table I.  QUALITIES CONSIDERED IMPORTANT FOR SUCCESS
LISTED BY AT LEAST 50 PER CENT OF THE SCHOOLS
AND COLLEGES REPLYING

| Teacher Training Institutions (13) | | School Administrators | | | |
|---|---|---|---|---|---|
| | | *Application Blanks* (25) | | *In-Service Rating Blanks* (22) | |
| QUALITY | % THAT MENTION | QUALITY | % THAT MENTION | QUALITY | % THAT MENTION |
| Appearance | 100 | Health | 92 | Human relations | 100 |
| Human relations | 85 | Teaching | | Understanding | |
| Ability to | | skill | 92 | children | 100 |
| communicate | 85 | Appearance | 84 | Health | 86 |
| Dependability | 85 | Human relations | 76 | Appearance | 86 |
| Response to | | Co-operation | 72 | Teaching skill | 86 |
| suggestions | 85 | Class | | Professional | |
| Professional | | management | 68 | growth | 82 |
| attitude | 77 | Personality | 64 | Class | |
| Voice | 77 | Professional | | management | 77 |
| Ability to organize | 69 | attitude | 64 | Dependability | 73 |
| Industry | 69 | Emotional | | Community | |
| Teaching skill | 62 | stability | 64 | relations | 73 |
| Initiative | 62 | Character | 60 | Interest in entire | |
| Health | 54 | Community | | school | 73 |
| Co-operation | 54 | relations | 52 | Professional | |
| Enthusiasm | 54 | | | attitude | 68 |
| Motor skill | 54 | | | Voice and ability to | |
| Resourcefulness | 54 | | | communicate | 68 |
| | | | | Friendly warmth | 68 |
| | | | | Knowledge of | |
| | | | | subject | 68 |
| | | | | Emotional | |
| | | | | stability | 64 |
| | | | | Routine duties | 64 |
| | | | | Democratic | |
| | | | | practice | 59 |
| | | | | Daily | |
| | | | | preparation | 55 |
| | | | | Enthusiasm | 50 |
| | | | | Public relations for | |
| | | | | school | 50 |

total school. Do the teacher training departments know what
the employers want and agree with them that these qualities are
important? Yes—on the whole. The college rating blanks have
some traits related to development in college, such as response
to suggestions, ability to organize, industry, initiative, and re-

sourcefulness. The last two, with motor skill, are particularly important in teaching physical education. Therefore they would be more likely to show upon department blanks than on the school blanks, which are used for all applicants.

A very well-known study of personality traits that children think are important in their teachers was made in connection with a radio contest. Describing "The Teacher Who Helped Me Most," some 1,400 children wrote letters to the sponsor. Here is their list of most important qualities: [1]

### Table II. QUALITIES FOUND HELPFUL BY CHILDREN

(in rank order of times mentioned)

1. Co-operative, democratic attitude
2. Kindliness and consideration of the individual
3. Patience
4. Wide interests
5. Personal appearance and pleasing manner
6. Fairness and impartiality
7. Sense of humor
8. Good disposition and consistent behavior
9. Interest in pupils' problems
10. Flexibility
11. . Use of recognition and praise
12. Unusual proficiency in teaching

Most of these traits spell out some of the details related to the more general terms used in the college and school blanks, such as human relations, personality, character, and understanding children. Like the administrators, in fact like almost everyone, children notice the teacher's appearance. Also they want skillful teachers, just as their elders do. They want teachers to have a sense of humor, which does not seem as im-

---

[1] Paul Witty, "An Analysis of the Personal Traits of an Effective Teacher," *Journal of Education Research,* **40** (May 1947), 662–71. By permission.

portant to those who train or employ teachers! A sense of humor, however, is one of six criteria used in a recent study to select a group of successful students and teachers. The other criteria were emotional maturity, extensive knowledge of subject matter, good health, pleasing personal appearance, and enthusiasm for work.[2] The author of the study states: "The qualities chosen as the criteria for success were selected after reviewing the research which has been done in that area by persons in education, physical education, psychology, and vocational guidance."

This, then, is the kind of person the college wants to have as a graduate, the superintendent wants to hire, and the child wants as his teacher. Are there many who meet these standards,

---

[2] Jo Ann Thorpe, "Study of Personality Variables Among Successful Women Students and Teachers of Physical Education," *Research Quarterly,* **29** (March 1958), 83.

### Democratic human relations

*State University of Iowa*

who rank high in all qualities? Certainly not; after all, teachers are human, and have human faults and foibles. However the prospective teacher should be reassured by knowing that successful persons are not all alike, but differ very much in appearance, personality patterns, degree of motor skill, and academic ability.

## Qualities observed in successful teachers and students of physical education

In appearance physical education teachers differ from each other just as members of any group do. Our favorite teacher in the third grade was a diminutive, black-eyed "fireball"; the next year we liked equally well a tall, blue-eyed blond of serene disposition. Watch the graduating physical education seniors at commencement: they may be tall, short, round faced, long faced, blond, or brunette; but most of them move well, stand well, and have a certain alert confidence, as if they knew what they were doing. The alumnae and teachers you will meet are also apt to have the good posture, good grooming, and directness characteristic of physical education graduates.

There is one more consideration about appearance that is very important for physical education teachers. Ever since the old days when love of sports was thought "tomboyish" or unladylike, there has persisted the stereotype of the boyish physical education teacher. The person with such a stereotype in mind may observe fifty attractive feminine youngsters on the athletic field and see only the fifty-first, a freckled faced crew-cut, huskily built girl. Ignoring the other fifty, the observer will say "now that's a typical physical education major."

If we want to correct this stereotype, and of course we do, since it is not a true picture of our group, we should take definite steps. First, each major should be *very* careful of her own hair-styling, her sports clothes, and her campus clothes. No jeans, slacks, or leotards for street or campus wear. Her sports clothes should be uniform, *clean,* and worn only for sports. Careful grooming is the rule. Hats, "heels 'n hose," and gloves are worn to church. Every major should study movement, in dance, sports, body mechanics or movement exploration classes, and try to develop fine carriage and a smooth walk (avoiding both the athlete's swagger and the model's hip-switch).

Suppose almost every one of the major group has made the most of her assets in looks, but one or two still cling to the small boy's indifference to cleanliness and scorn of appearances. Can the majority help the "tomboys" to arrive at a better attitude? They should try, if they do not want all majors to be judged by these few. There are many ways of approaching the problem: through departmental advisers, through major club programs or role playing in class, through talks by local school administrators, who are always glad to comment on the teacher's appearance, and through discussions in housing groups.

Another approach is to publicize the most charming looking major students. The means of doing this will depend on the local campus situation. In one large university where "queens" were elected in profusion, the major department voted for queens in every line of their work: queen of baseball, of field hockey, of archery, and of other sports. Pictures were portraits, *not* in sports clothes, and the girls were photogenic queens!

Department social functions, coffee hours for visiting dignitaries or local faculty guests, the annual senior banquet, and occasional dances, give other opportunities for good publicity pictures, and should be well reported in the campus paper. Other campus social functions will give majors occasion to know more people, have more fun, and to represent their department to advantage. Each major should remember that to make the most of her looks, is to help change whatever unfavorable and untrue stereotype may be prevalent on her campus.

In personality patterns, that is, the individual's feelings and actions as observed in his social setting, we find great diversity among physical education majors and teachers. However, there are certain characteristics which seem to distinguish the successful ones from the general run of persons tested. The physical education groups tend to be more outgoing, open to suggestion, willing to accept the leadership of others, while at the same time they are likely to be selected as leaders by their peers. They are good organizers and definitely superior in their ability to work long hours at a job until it is finished. They are less apt to be aggressively unconventional and nonconforming, less given to personal dependence on others, and less the "clinging vine" in their relations with males.[3]

Outside interests of physical education students and teachers include sports, of course, and other forms of active recreation such as dance, camping, and outings. A brief survey of hobbies of teachers in our field indicates a long list of less active pursuits: music, reading, radio, television, painting, ceramics and other arts and crafts, theater, photography, gardening, cooking, social and civic clubs, and various activities in connection with church membership and church attendance. In other words, these persons have many interests. They enjoy and continue participating in sports longer than most women do. They like to work in groups, but find many resources of an individual nature for their leisure time at home.

Skills are related to interests: we tend to choose for our work and for our recreation those things we do well. Therefore we would expect women in physical education to be skilled in sports and dance. This does not mean that they have the top-flight skill needed in tournament play or concert dance that comes with long years of specialization. It does mean that they are above the average of college women in the sports they know

---

[3] Thorpe, *op.cit.* p. 85.

and also in their ability to learn new sports. By the end of their course they have developed a good degree of teaching skill. For teaching, the ability to perform helps, but it is not as important as the ability to understand, to guide, and to encourage the learning of others.

Community relationships play an important part in the lives of physical education students and teachers. The college is the students' community, and they take part in large and small

Fencing takes control and speed

group organizations.[4] Teachers find time for Scouts, PTA groups, religious interests, service clubs, civic organizations, and social and sport clubs. With their outgoing tendencies and ability to work with others, either as group members or leaders, they usually are assured of respect in the community and a large circle of friends and acquaintances.

[4] See Chap. 4 and 5.

Health records of women physical education teachers are better than average. Absenteeism is low, and incidence of organic disease is low. Part of this may be explained by selection at the college level. If medical examinations at entrance or during the course detect health deficiency, the student does not enter or continue in the physical education course. Another favorable factor is physical activity continued beyond college to a greater degree than is common with women in general. The beneficial effects of exercise are too well known to need stressing at this point; undoubtedly they do contribute to the good health of women in this profession. A third favorable factor is good mental health. The extrovert, well adjusted to her situation, working in a profession she enjoys, able to see the progress her students are making, and convinced that this progress is important to their development, has every chance for sound mental health. While this picture may not describe every teacher in this field, it is true of enough of them to explain the fact that incidence of psychoneurosis is comparatively low among the group members.

Academic ability is important to the career of any teacher, although it may not affect progress in the first few years as much as it does later. Sometimes the idea gets around that physical skill and high grades do not go together: the "dumb athlete" is a stereotype found more often in fiction than in fact. True, the highly specialized athletic champion may often give too much of his time to his specialization, be it basketball, swimming, golf, or baseball, and not enough time to study or to develop good work habits in school. But present-day research nevertheless shows the academic average of this group (majors in health, physical education, and recreation) near the college average.

The most conspicuous cause of failure on any job, and especially in teaching physical education, seems to be lack of ability to get along with others. While this is found rather infrequently in physical education groups, it has characterized a few, who usually leave teaching for other work. However, if brilliant in lecturing, research work, or writing, the less well-adjusted teacher may achieve a measure of success, but her accomplishments would be doubled or tripled if she were easy to work with. This is one reason why *all* rating blanks ask for information about human relations.

Integrity is the qualification most highly prized by one staff group asked to draw up standards for selection of new staff members. They thought it basic to group morale and to student confidence. It is a hard word to define, but as this group talked about it the concept evolved of a person whose ideas, ideals, and actions are consistent and reliable. "She said that she'd do it, and you can count on that." "She wears well." "Just as good as she looks, and that's really good." Or, negatively, "A smoothie." "All things to all people." "Will never come right out and say what she believes." "She doesn't always stick to the facts; can't be sure of what she says."

Understanding other people and intuitive response to their needs is perhaps the outstanding characteristic of the "born teacher." This is the teacher who has just the right word and action in any discipline situation, who knows how to channel the school child's enthusiasm and how to stimulate enthusiasm of older, less active students. Is this an innate quality? Is it entirely intuitive? Can it be developed? Yes, no, and yes. That is to say, yes, some persons are naturally equipped with it; no, it is not always a quick, sure response; yes, it may be developed by trial and observation or study. In study, perhaps the most helpful principle to attempt to apply is the Ethical Imperative stated long ago by Kant, the great German philosopher: "Treat humanity, in yourself or others, as an end always, never as a means only." That is to say, do not *use* the child, nor let him impose on you. Try to understand what he *needs* at the moment of stress, whether it be firm but kindly regulation or warm acceptance and praise.

Drive toward a professional goal gives direction as well as

"steam" to the teacher's efforts. Many of the rating blanks call this industry, or professional attitude, but such expressions can only approximate what is meant. The case of a young woman known to the author (the name of the woman is fictitious), illustrates this drive:

Mary Nolan was a warm-hearted, good-looking, Irish girl, whose easy wit and human qualities made her a favorite with her classmates. She was right at the bottom of the list in academic entrance tests, but was full of enthusiasm, highly skilled in sports, and determined to graduate and to teach physical education. Her determination was well tested in her freshman year. At the end of the first semester she had one failure, three D's and one B. But she persisted. Any odd moment between classes found Mary in the library. She took to bringing her lunch and taking a long solitary noon-hour of study in the department library. In the late afternoon she played club hockey, basketball, or tennis. In the evenings she was back in the library.

She did graduate. No one but Mary and her advisers knew the amount of effort represented by that C average. In her first teaching position she was tested all over again. The school board had been elected on an economy platform. They attacked first the special subjects: music, art, home economics, shop, and physical education, with the slogan "Back to the three R's." Mary was immediately successful with her classes. With the help of the high-school girls she begged old tennis rackets and golf clubs from door to door, so they might have beginning instruction in these popular sports with no additional cost to the school. She persuaded the service clubs to finance treatment for physically handicapped children. When the program was well established her students were asked to fill out questionnaires evaluating all phases of it, including controversial issues such as showers, excuses, and clean uniforms. Their approval in a high percentage of responses gave her renewed confidence and good evidence when she was asked to come before the Board of Education, as she was several different times during the year. At the end of the year she was one of the few special subjects teachers reappointed; her salary was increased, and her request for a supply budget was approved—all by an economy minded board. "Drive" took her through a very hard year with great credit, and saw physical education more firmly established than before in her school.

The student is advised to remember always that no one can rate high in all qualities. If a student is in good health, likes activities, enjoys working with people and with ideas, she has a good start. While no prospective teacher should try to fit her own personality into another's pattern, a smart student will know her own strengths and weaknesses and act accordingly. If she can use the information in this chapter as a guide to chart her own progress, she'll be making an intelligent approach to success in her work.

### QUESTIONS

1. Could you make out a self-rating blank? Do you think it would help or hinder your development in college?

2. Among your friends who are not majoring in physical education are there some who would rate high on any of the three blanks described in the chapter? Would it help them if you brought to their attention the fact that they might be successful in the field?

3. Which traits in Table I are most clear to you? Least clear?

4. Explain the meaning of "personality pattern."

5. Try dramatizing a situation in which several applicants for a summer camp job are being interviewed; one of them is very boyish in manner and appearance. (Have a very feminine girl play this role.)

6. Does it make any difference what socially approved hobbies a physical education teacher has? A recreation leader?

7. Can you distinguish between skill in swimming and skill in teaching swimming? Which seems more important to you?

8. Try rating your most successful high school teachers of physical education on the in-service rating blank in Table I.

9. In the case of "Mary Nolan," do you think it was "drive" that made her successful? What other traits helped her?

10.  Divide the class into small groups and request a short interview for each group with a local school official in which you find out what he thinks the most important qualifications for the kind of work you want to do. Report back to class.

11.  When you meet a new acquaintance who says on hearing of your major: "Well, you don't look it!" what do you answer? See if the class can make up an answer that shows loyalty to the group and skill in counteracting the stereotype.

12.  Has this chapter helped you in any way? Explain.

### SELECTED REFERENCES

Bucher, Charles A. *Foundations of Physical Education,* 2nd ed. (St. Louis: Mosby, 1956), Chap. 14.

Davis, Elwood C., and John D. Lawther. *Successful Teaching in Physical Education,* 2nd ed. (Englewood Cliffs, New Jersey: Prentice-Hall, 1948), Chap. 22.

Halsey, Elizabeth, and Lorena Porter. *Physical Education for Children: A Developmental Program* (New York: Dryden-Holt, 1958), Chap. V.

Joint Committee on Health Problems in Education. Washington: National Education Association, 1959.

Williams, Jesse F. *Principles of Physical Education,* 7th ed. (Philadelphia: Saunders, 1959), Chap. I.

# CHAPTER 3

# *Success in Homemaking*

IN THEIR YEARS OF college living, young men and women face many problems related to the future. Some are the same for both: How do I prepare for my job or my profession? What general courses will give me a liberal education, making living more interesting for me and making me a more interesting person? What kind of life partner am I going to marry? Other problems differ because men and women have different roles in our society. Women still have the main responsibility for homemaking. It is true that men contribute a great deal to life in the home beyond financial support; in the modern, servantless, appliance-served household, many of them share household tasks to an extent undreamed of by previous generations. This is more often the case, of course, when the wife also is employed outside the home. But whether she is an employed worker or a busy housewife, the woman is likely to have the chief responsibility for such matters as the warmth or chill of the family atmosphere, the relaxation or tension of interpersonal relations, the attractiveness or discomfort of the home setting, the smoothness or disorders of the daily program. Hers also are the very practical jobs of feeding the family wisely, spending for daily needs, and planning developmental recreation.[1] These aspects of family living have great influence on family health and security, not only for the children but for the parents as well. The college woman who wishes to face her future role as homemaker realistically, prepares for homemaking as well as for her career.

## Study of physical education graduates who marry

One of the early objections to college education for women was that it would "unfit" them for marriage. Men, it was argued, would not want intellectual wives, and college women would not want the nonintellectual job of being a housewife. The course of events has dispelled this fear; the trend is toward earlier marriages of college graduates, and less of a differential among various educational levels in the percentage of women who marry. In 1950 a study was made of several hundred women who had received the B.A. degree with specialization in physical education at the State University of Iowa, from 1924 to 1950. A part of the study dealt with the marital status of those who had been out of college ten years or more, as reported in Table III.

Table III.   MARITAL STATUS OF B.A. GRADUATES
TEN YEARS AFTER GRADUATION [a]

| Status | Number | Percentage |
|--------|--------|------------|
| Married (one or more times) * | 117 | 77 |
| Divorced | 3 | 2 |
| Widowed | 3 | 2 |
| Single | 35 | 23 |

[a] Classes 1924–39. Total: $N = 152$.
* Including these now widowed or divorced.

Of these women, 77 per cent were married. The figure for all women graduates of the Liberal Arts College for the same

[1] Developmental recreation entails constructive activities leading to healthy mental and emotional as well as physical growth.

period was reported by the alumni office as 78 per cent married. The average number of children for the families that had them was 2.1, compared with the figure of 2.0 for the general group. The divorce rate in the Iowa study (2 per cent) is very low in comparison with other reports. The rate for college graduates as a whole is usually given as 7 per cent. Studies of the total population by Kingsley Davis, reported in 1950, gives the divorce rate per 100 marriages occurring in the previous ten years. The rate fluctuates from 5.1 in 1881 to 40.1 in 1946, and down to 22.1 in 1950.[2] Jacobson found that the divorce rate was related to the number of children.[3] In Table IV compiled from Davis' findings, we see that couples with no children had a divorce rate of 15.3 per cent, those with children, 8.8 per cent. When grouped according to the number of children, the divorce rate seemed to decrease as the families grew, those with four children having a rate of only 4.6 per cent.

Table IV. DIVORCES OF MARRIED COUPLES ACCORDING TO SIZE OF FAMILY

| Number of Children (under 18) | Per Cent Divorced |
| --- | --- |
| 0 | 15.3 |
| 1 | 11.6 |
| 2 | 7.6 |
| 3 | 6.5 |
| 4 | 4.6 |
| Total with children | 8.8 |

## Factors in marital happiness

Although divorce is generally considered evidence of marital maladjustment, there are many other approaches to the study

[2] Kingsley Davis, "Divorce and Its Effects," in Morris Fishbein and Ruby Jo Reeves Kennedy, *Modern Marriage and Family Living* (New York: Oxford, 1957), p. 108.
[3] Paul H. Jacobson, "Differentials in Divorce," *American Sociological Review,* 15 (April 1950), 235–44.

of adjustment in marriage, and the factors contributing to its success or failure. Many well-known authorities, after a great deal of research on this problem, believe they can predict the future happiness of engaged couples.[4] Although they do not claim accuracy in each individual case, general trends do appear, and many students will be interested in considering the things which make for or against happiness in marriage.

Background during the childhood and youth of both husband and wife seems to be important. Favorable aspects are:

1. A happy childhood in a large family with attachment to both parents, and firm but not harsh discipline.

2. Similarity of cultural backgrounds, i.e., occupation of father, nationality, educational and income level of parents as well as religious participation, social status, and frank attitudes toward sex.

Several adult situational conditions favoring marital adjustment are identified:

1. Common interests and values that lead to the essential factor of companionship. "For a happy union the prospective husband and wife must participate together in a sufficient number of activities that insure companionship. Their mutual activities and interests may be in sports and games, literature, music and art, or religion and a social cause." [5]

2. Social participation (varied interests, many friends, and belonging to organizations) indicates a good marriage risk.

3. Religious participation contributes more than mere affiliation with a church.

4. Level of education and maturity has a positive relation-

---

[4] See Ernest W. Burgess and Leonard S. Cottrell Jr., *Predicting Success or Failure in Marriage* (New York: Prentice-Hall, 1939); and Lewis M. Terman, *Psychological Factors in Marital Happiness* (New York: McGraw-Hill, 1938).

[5] Ernest W. Burgess, "The Wise Choice of a Mate," in Fishbein and Kennedy, *op.cit.,* p. 126. By permission.

ship. That is, the more highly educated the better the chance of married happiness, and later marriages seem to be more successful than very early ones.

5. Sexual compatibility is rated as an important factor by most authorities. Nimkoff, however, thinks that perhaps it has been overrated as an essential factor. He states that it does not always lead to happy marriage, nor does lack of it always cause unhappy marriage.[6]

6. Strong desire for children and great interest in children and the home on the part of both husband and wife contribute to happiness.

7. Economic status: it is not shown that there is an increase in adjustment with increase of income above the moderate level necessary for security.

8. Occupation: stability and social control (through the force of community opinion) seem favorable; teachers, ministers, and engineers appear to be better risks than salesmen, laborers, and mechanics. Wives who work before or after marriage have a good chance of adjustment if attitudes are considered. If the wife is working in an occupation she likes, and if she wants to work, she has a better chance for adjustment than if she wants to work but doesn't. Of course the husband's attitude toward his wife's work is very important.[7]

Personality patterns of husband and wife are extremely important. Findings of an early study by Lewis Terman were interpreted by him as indicating that certain types of personality could never make satisfactory adjustments in marriage.[8] He concluded that the nervous, oversensitive, contentious, unfriendly, restless, unsystematic, and unconventional woman feels insecure in the marriage situation (as in almost any other

---

[6] Meyer F. Nimkoff, *Marriage and the Family* (Boston: Houghton Mifflin, 1947), p. 200.

[7] Nimkoff, *op.cit.*, p. 498.

[8] Terman, *op.cit.*, Chap. 7.

demanding relationship) and shows her feelings in various ways which cause unhappiness. It may be what Terman calls a "flight into reality," that is, a restless drive to community participation not so much to serve, as to gain recognition for herself. Or it may be extramarital searching for romantic interest contributing to self-buildup. According to Terman the man with similar personality traits is more apt to withdraw from community participation and to develop hostility toward all women.

Later case studies of married couples show that the interaction of their personalities is more important than the individual personality patterns of husband and wife, and that compatibility of wishes is essential to their adjustment.[9]

Burgess summarizes the personality factor by saying that the characteristics associated with happiness are optimism, emotional stability, submissive rather than domineering tendencies, considerateness and sympathy, self-confidence rather than lack of it, and emotional dependence rather than self-sufficiency. If both husband and wife have these characteristics, there is the best chance for marital success; if neither one has them the chance is poor; if lacks in one are supplemented by positive qualities in the other, there is a moderate chance.[10]

These studies by Burgess and Terman, and the one by Thorpe discussed in Chapter 2, indicate that some of the traits favorable to marital happiness also characterize successful physical education majors and teachers. The author would like to add observations from long contact with married graduates of physical education and recreation courses; from visits in their homes, chats with their families as they came back to the campus, written communication from them, and friendship over a period of years.

---

[9] Nimkoff, *op.cit.,* p. 484.
[10] E. W. Burgess, "The Wise Choice of a Mate," in Fishbein and Kennedy, *op.cit.,* p. 124.

Three qualities stand out. First is a certain buoyancy: the anticipation of fun, and the ability to have fun in almost any situation. The French call it *joie de vivre*. Whether it comes from the euphoria of good health, from the love of activity, or from more mysterious inner sources of gaiety is not important. It seems to be a built-in, priceless gift, characteristic of our group.

Second, and closely related to the first, is what might be called a durable but flexible aptitude for companionship. This means companionship with husband and with children, both outdoors and indoors, in active sports and less active interests like reading, music, and crafts. A major learns to be companionable in the close group contacts of her own class, her teams, and her clubs.

When the "going gets rough" the third quality comes out. To "take it" without self-pity is certaintly well-learned in sports; tested by a hockey ball on the shins, or loss of a crucial basketball game, and no whining in either case. It is a great boon to the homecoming husband if his wife has met domestic problems competently, and can understate them humorously in the telling. It is a great discomfort if she dwells on disaster stories, or begs for sympathy with daily accounts of pains and aches.

These qualities, so it seems, are gifts that lighten any family living: fun, companionship, and stability in rough domestic weather. The author believes that most majors in our field have them.

## Other aspects of successful family living

In addition to the mutual happiness of husband and wife, favorable development of children is an obvious criterion of successful family living. When children first attend preschool, kindergarten, or first grade they are beginning their "schooling," but their informal education began at birth. The teacher may interpret the quality of a child's home education by the degree of his security, his physical and mental health, and the status of his development.

What kind of a home produces secure, healthy, well-developed children? Several factors contribute.

Parents' acceptance of and love for their children, illuminated by understanding of the facts of child development are the first essential. Parental love gives the child that anchor of security which comes from knowing that he is wanted, that he will never be rejected, and that his home is a "port of refuge." Parental understanding of the child's capacities and limitations makes possible a sensible framework of discipline and a reasonably ordered regime of living in which cause and effect, action and consequences are consistently related. This also is basic to the child's sense of security. If he forgets about safety rules, and on one occasion is punished for playing with matches but gets by with an irritated reprimand the next time, all rules take on uncertainty. If promises are forgotten by parents, and threats left unfulfilled, if mother dissolves in tears, or father storms in uncontrolled temper, the child's world is shaken by loss of faith in adult justice, strength, and stability. Again the child's sense of security is damaged.

A warm social climate is more important to a home than the even physical warmth of modern central heating. (Unfortunately there is no family thermostat that can regulate the ups and downs of bickering among a group of rugged individuals.) It is the basic warmth of affection among members of the family, and friendship for the close associates who enjoy the hospitality of the home, that provide the comfort of a relaxed atmosphere. Hospitality is expressed in the very appearance of such a home: it looks as if people lived in it with pleasure and cared for it with interest. Beauty is evident, but not perfection of order or too many "conversation pieces" too fragile for use. There may or may not be a family room, but every room welcomes some members of the family for its particular function.

Living religion, which the child may be led to see in everyday situations—at his own level of insight—contributes greatly to the warmth of family living. Conventional church affiliation that does not go beyond Sabbath observance is not as potent a factor as active participation in church life and use of religious teaching in everyday life.

The homemaker should be aware of another factor that may have a positive or negative effect on the ease of interpersonal relations in the home. In a competitive culture such as ours, members of the family are constantly in situations of stress outside the home. Children compete in school for grades, for the attention and approval of the teacher, to win games, class elections, and even in the daily situation of acceptance or rejection by their peers. Adults work under strenuous competition to outdistance the rest of the work force or their job specifications, to outsell others in their field, and to outsmart any and all rivals. However stimulating these attitudes of rivalry may be in work situations, they tend to destroy warm family feeling and to produce stress instead of relaxation when brought into home living. If the wife is critical of her husband's activities, if she "cuts him down to size" instead of building him up, she is depriving him of the emotional security he needs and should find in his home. Conversely, a husband who speaks patronizingly of his wife's homemaking accomplishments, or takes them for granted without a word of recognition, and who is sarcastic about her community work, club or social life, merely adds to the frustration she may feel as she contemplates her so-called "trivial world." If both work, and both carry competitive work habits into their marital relations, the results according to Landis are disastrous: "Affection evaporates, and the marriage becomes comparable to business relationship with the same ruthless driving for success, the same quest for recognition. As love dies the craving for status and recognition becomes more desperate." [11] Marriage, he states, should be an institution of close complementary co-operation rather than competition.

Children are still more vulnerable than adults to the cutting edge of competition, because their protection through emotional maturity develops slowly. If a child is continually urged to "get good grades like Tommy" or if he feels that the new baby is now getting all the attention while he himself is neglected, his own self-confidence diminishes. At this stage he often withdraws from the family circle, which is not good, or he may use "attention getting" devices that are still worse. When report cards are brought home parental wisdom is put to a severe test. Too often comments run something like this: "Why did you only get a C in spelling? That's an easy subject." "Aren't you just as bright as the Blake boy? His mother told me he got straight A's." "Let's see: two A's, that's 50 cents added to your allowance, one B—you break even on that, two C's is 20 cents off and one D is 25 cents off. So you get a nickel more this time. It will sure pay you to try for more A's—no, I don't want any excuses." (All this may be said to a child of only average ability!) Some modern schools seek to minimize this competitive stress and give more meaningful information by using descriptive reports of various aspects of the child's school performance that are designed to help parents understand the child's progress. However in many instances schools abandon the plan because parents are accustomed to grades and want this more definite evaluation. It is the rare parent who can help the child take a realistic look at his report card and review his progress. "What do you think of your C in spelling, son? Does an inventor need to spell accurately? Suppose you were head of a big research station and got letters of application from young men—would a few misspelled words make any difference? How do you plan to work at this?" If the child is helped to relate

---

[11] Paul H. Landis, *Making the Most of Marriage* (New York: Appleton-Century-Crofts, 1955), p. 293.

his progress to his own plans he will have a more consistent urge to effort than he might get from any temporary rivalry.

Experience in athletics may help in homemaking. If the mother has played games and had fun at it the chances are that she doesn't take competition as a life-or-death matter. That is, she may be a keen competitor but not a bitter loser. Moreover, if she is something of a philosopher and understands what rivalry does to her children (and herself) and what undercutting might do to her husband, she will keep these intense forms of competition away from the home and fireside. Such desirable attitudes, say most women leaders in physical education and recreation, should be a planned outcome of the sports program. They are quite sure this can be done more readily in intramural contests than when the intense pressures of varsity-type games build up. Understanding and controlling

## Fun for to-day and for many to-morrows

State University of Iowa

competition is one of the persistent problems in physical education and recreation. The reader will meet it again in later chapters.

The family's recreation may also help or hinder the child's
development. In addition it has been found to be a factor in
parents' mutual compatibility through shared interests. Constructive recreation requires good planning by parents because
there is available a great deal of useless low cost entertainment
that may at times be more harmful than useless. Constructive
recreation is "active, creative, varied, and sociable." It gives at
least some of the following results: [12]

1.  Enjoyment and satisfaction
2.  Physical activity
3.  Outlet for aggressive feelings
4.  Exploration of new experiences; this in turn gives new
    learnings, growth, and breadth of understanding
5.  Full expression of personality
6.  Attaining some sort of success
7.  Social contacts with individuals and groups
8.  Occasional escape from reality
9.  Creative achievement
10. Service to the community
11. Strengthening of moral and ethical codes

Admittedly it is a tax on the ingenuity of parents to get these
outcomes for small children weatherbound within a small
house. If the father can plan a well-lighted, dry, cheerful recreation room in the basement, and if the mother can organize her
schedule so as to give some companionship and supervision
while the children are playing downstairs, the activity and space
problem will be helped. In addition, parents should explore the
resources of their own communities; not only organized programs but also natural attractions such as picnic spots, fishing

---

[12] *Developing Democratic Human Relationships,* First Yearbook (Washington: AAHPER), p. 362.

holes, and hiking trails. Many of the references at the end of this chapter will give detailed suggestions, and members of local child study groups will exchange useful information about family recreation. All persons who have studied children agree that parents should not depend on the cheap and easy mass media: television, radio, comics, and movies, but should use the very limited number of better programs with discrimination and should give their families more memorable fun through family outings as well as shared interests and activities at home. Among the most important shared interests are reading, music, and creative arts and crafts. Reading aloud, library visits, Christmas gifts of books or money for the purchase of books, start children on ever-expanding worlds of interests. Shared family music, and dramatics, even if not on expert levels, may contribute to lasting appreciation. Drawing, painting, modeling, and crafts are messy but very satisfying things for children to do.

Parents who are good companions remember that every child needs an audience for understanding and appreciation; every child needs times of working with playmates and times when he can be happy working alone. To him the main point is acceptance and interest.

Fortunately, constructive recreation can be economically planned to fit into a limited budget. Stoutly constructed, home-built or improvised apparatus for the backyard or the basement recreation room may provide more developmental activity than the traditional gym sets.[13] Utility balls of rubber or other comparatively cheap materials are as good as leather for informal play. Homemade game sets for bean bag target throws, darts, shuffle board, tether ball, and others make fine do-it-yourself projects for the older members of the family.

The homemaker who has kept a notebook in her college courses on play and recreation will find help here.

---

[13] Elizabeth Halsey and Lorena Porter, *Physical Education for Children: A Developmental Program* (New York: Holt, 1958), Chap. 6.

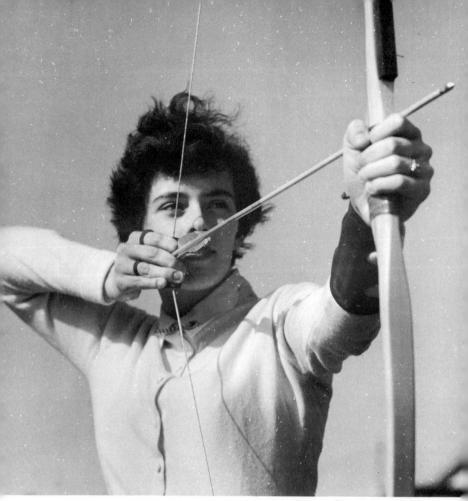

Archery gives enjoyment and satisfaction

Thus a limited income does not in itself limit the quality of the family's recreation, nor the success or happiness of family living—not unless it is so low that there is insecurity and tension between parents, or the mother is forced into outside work when no adequate adult care can be provided for the children. The feeling of insecurity is not always related to the actual income level. This is partly a matter of the parents' mental hygiene, and may be modified as they learn to face reality and to plan more carefully. Thrifty buying, with built-up resistance to "hidden persuaders," home construction of clothing and food, the kind of budgeting which plans for cash rather than installment buying and other exorbitant interest payments, will help in achieving the feeling as well as the substance of economic security. To succeed at this wise and careful planning the homemaker must learn to stay out of social competition; i.e., "keeping up with the Joneses" who may have twice her income.

The family's health, however, should not be an economy item. There is no do-it-yourself, or learn-it-from-the-neighbors substitute for the trained physician's diagnosis and prescription. However, there are important local differences in the amount of help available to families of limited means. Various kinds of group insurance are provided for employees in different companies, institutions, or organizations. Low-cost community clinics open to the public are often operated in connection with medical schools. Such opportunities are worth investigating when considering job offers. There is also the program of disease prevention and positive health which the parents provide in the home; it may be effective or not depending on the soundness of their information and planning. Feeding the family properly is of prime importance, and the science of nutrition is not picked up casually by trial and error in the kitchen. Periodic dental and medical examinations, and preventive immunizations are good investments. Co-operation in school health measures and in school programs in health, physical education, and safety education are important to children's health. The child's mental health will be favorably affected by many factors previously described: the security of stability, warmth, affection, freedom from competitive stresses, and the happiness of shared family recreation.

The child's habits of sleep, eating, cleanliness and exercise are the product of early home training; they are, of course, basic to his future health. Safety factors in the home environment must be understood by parents and children alike; safety rules must be carefully made and obeyed.

## Homemaking and/or careers

In the nineteenth century women had no chice: they were either homemakers or maiden aunt baby sitters depending on circumstances. At the beginning of the twentieth century, women had to make a choice between homemaking and a career, and very few of them chose careers. But both men and women were in jobs if they could get them during the depression, and when World War II came all the country went to work. Not many women of your generation will miss the experience of holding a paid job and meeting job competence standards.[14] Many social and economic changes aside from war have produced this revolution in the work force of our society. These changes will be treated at greater length in Chapter 7. It is enough now to recognize that economic expansion demanded more workers than the increasing male population could provide, and that social traditions restricting the field of women's activities changed as women responded to the greater demand for workers.

Since most women graduates of college will have some sort of paid position either before or during marriage, it seems pertinent to consider how work outside the home affects success in homemaking. We have already seen that the wife's work experience may be favorable to marital happiness if she works at the type of job she likes. However, it is frustrating for a young woman to give up her own professional course after a year or two of study; then marry, and take a routine job to support herself and her husband while he finishes his professional training. The other pattern, described in the first chapter

---

[14] *Spotlight on Women in the U. S.* (Washington: Women's Bureau, U.S. Bureau of Labor, 1958), p. 8.

by "Dorothy Hale McDowell," in which the wife marries after she has finished college and then teaches to add to the family income, often works out well—at least till the children appear. What then? Popular debate has been voluminous and vociferous on both sides of this question, but statistics show that most women recognize the demands of small children and drop out of the work force if they are financially able to do so. In 1957 only one out of five mothers of preschool children was working, while two out of five mothers who had school-age children only, were working.[15] The problem for the mother whose children are away all day at school is to decide whether she can organize her housework, give up community and social activities, plan her job schedule so as to be home when the children come in from school, and have the physical stamina to take on a double responsibility: paid work and homemaking.

**Contributions to the community.** If the homemaker decides against paid work, she will probably become involved in more forms of community service. Health, physical education and recreation graduates are exceptionally well equipped for volunteer leadership in hospitals, scouting, "Y" work, or community-center programs. Most of them take some active part in PTA's, church work, women's clubs, or other civic enterprises. Temperamentally, as we have seen, they enjoy groups and work well with people. Their chief problem seems to be in selecting among many demands, and in scheduling organization appointments so as to leave time for their main job of homemaking. The homemaker who has "kept her hand in" community affairs is ready to make an easy adaptation to the time when her children are grown and on their own, leaving the mother with days which might otherwise seem as empty as her house. This is the time when she can do a big job—either for pay or for service—if she is equipped and ready to do so.

---

[15] *1958 Handbook on Women Workers* (Washington: Women's Bureau, U.S. Department of Labor, 1958), p. 40.

**Unmarried career women and their homes.** Characteristically, single women who work want to establish themselves in a homelike situation as soon as possible. After living for a year or so in a room, most young teachers will expand into an apartment or house shared with one or more friends. As they pool financial resources and homemaking talents, and divide responsibility for meals and housework, the result is often a very attractive living situation. The very impermanence of such an arrangement may lend it a certain casual charm, and it may well serve as apprentice training for the more serious business of married family life. Those career women who do not marry usually evolve permanent and satisfying patterns of home living. As their financial positions improve their homes become more attractive, and they are often ready and able to assume responsibility for parents or other near relatives. Whatever the constituency of the unmarried career woman's "family" (friends, colleagues, dependent or independent relatives) the happiness of members of the household is affected by the same factors that apply in any home life: warm social atmosphere, hospitality, charm and informality of home decoration, shared recreation and interests, and freedom from the tension of intrafamily competition.

**College as education for homemaking.** Obviously the college woman majoring in physical education and allied fields should accept the fact that she will at some time be a homemaker. In all probability she will marry and have children. For these important responsibilities she needs the best preparation college can give her. Three sources for this preparation are available to her: professional courses in her major, electives, and extracurricular experiences. Her professional courses will give her information about child development and health; physical education activities and recreation for all ages; field work in group leadership and practice teaching experience with children; psychology of learning and adjustment; mental health

—and many other things important to family living. In departments of Home Economics she may elect among courses in nutrition (a must), home management, food preparation, art in the home, textiles, and others. In sociology she will look for courses in marriage and the family, community organization, human nature and personality, and others interpreting group experience. In fact, she will have to select from a wealth of course offerings rather than to hunt for something appropriate. Extracurricular activities will give experience in individual sports, group leadership, social recreation, community service, dating and courtship, and organization of work-study-play schedules. If she must earn money, it might be good sense to consider child care and baby-sitting jobs, or working for her board and room with a well-recommended family. The insight into family relationships provided by this last type of job is extremely valuable. Summer work as a camp counselor or recreation leader will be useful. All of these experiences will interest the college student in relation to her future needs, and, in turn, make her a more interesting person in the present.

## QUESTIONS

1. In your opinion do most college students think about marriage as a certainty? As a probability? As a problem?

2. If the study quoted (marital status of physical education alumnae) were to be repeated today would you expect the results to differ? What is the reason for your answer?

3. Would you expect the divorce rate for physical education graduates to be higher, lower, or the same as that for other college graduates?

4. From your observations which set of factors would you say are most important to marital happiness: childhood background, adult situational factors, adult personality patterns? Why?

5. List the advantages for homemaking that your major provides.

6. Do you expect to teach before you marry? After you marry? After you have children? What situation might change your present decision?

7. Do you think most parents you have observed understand child development?

8. What other aspects of successful family living do these parents practice most? Least?

9. Is it especially important for physical education majors to understand the effect of competition, co-operation, and recreation in the home?

10. Try role playing to illustrate two different family atmospheres: in one the atmosphere is intensely competitive; in the other competition is deliberately reduced or "soft-pedaled" by the parents. Have the same students play the same roles in the two contrasting situations.

11. What family recreation did you enjoy most as a child?

12. Do you expect to participate in your family's recreation during vacations this year? Are you learning anything at college which may help in this respect?

13. Do you have the opportunity to observe a child under twelve in such a way that you could analyze how home conditions are affecting his development either favorably or unfavorably?

14. Comment on at least three factors contributing to the changes in women's employment during the past forty years.

15. What are your plans for improving your preparation for homemaking?

## SELECTED REFERENCES

Carlson, Reynold E.: "The Family Camping Boom," *Journal AAHPER*, 30 No. 5 (May-June 1959), 33.

Force, Elizabeth: *Your Family Today and Tomorrow* (New York: Harcourt Brace, 1955).

Gruenberg, Sidonie, and Hilda Sidney Krech. *The Many Lives of Modern Woman* (New York: Doubleday, 1952), Chap. IV and V.

Mueller, Kate Hevner. *Educating Women for a Changing World* (Minneapolis: University of Minnesota Press, 1954), Chap. VI and IX.

Rice, Thurman B. and Fred V. Hein. *Living* rev. ed. (Chicago: Scott Foresman, 1954), Chap. X.

Stoddard, George D. *On the Education of Women* (New York: Macmillan, 1920), Chap. III.

Turner, C. E. *Personal and Community Health,* 11th ed. (St. Louis: Mosby, 1959), Chap. XIX.

Witmer, Helen Leland, and Ruth Kotinsky. *Personality in the Making* (New York: Harper, 1952), Chap. IX.

# CHAPTER 4

# *Professional Preparation:*

## GENERAL TRENDS

WHILE COLLEGE WOMEN know they will need preparation for homemaking, as discussed in the last chapter, most of them consider their first concern to be preparing for a job, or a profession. Most of the readers of this book plan to teach physical education or health education; some will go into a graduate course in physical therapy; and some will become recreation leaders. All will deal with children and youth and must know a great deal about them and how they develop, socially and emotionally as well as mentally and physically. Both teachers and recreation leaders will be living and working in this society: the United States today. They should, then, understand our particular pattern of culture and the place of the school or recreation agency in that culture. Moreover, all college students are privileged to enter a world of understanding with ways of thinking and meeting problems that characterize the "educated" person. In addition, of course, they will need the great body of special information and technical skills that makes them proficient in their special fields. Most colleges today advise students to balance their common needs with their professional goals, by taking general as well as specialized courses. As a rule, general education comes fairly early in the college program, and professional education later on—although there will be introductory professional experiences which identify the beginning student with her major department and also some general courses in the junior and senior years.

## Basic requirements for different types of work

The pattern of general education as most colleges plan it is made up of certain skills and understandings. Skills of communication include reading, writing, and speaking clearly, correctly, and expressively. Skills in the use of abstract symbols and mathematical processes, and in the effective use of bodily movement, are also included in many college programs of general education. To understand human beings is the goal of such areas as the biological sciences, psychology, and the expressive arts. Understanding society and the impact of our culture upon human beings comes from the social sciences, history, the humanities, religion, philosophy and ethics. Understanding our physical environment involves earth science, physical science, the study of cosmic phenomena such as space and the planetary and solar systems. All freshmen are exposed to general education. If they are desirous of converting exposure to a deeper experience, they may "catch" the characteristics of the person who is free from the limitations and prejudices we associate with lack of education. This catching process means hard work.

In addition to general education, beginners in the three lines of work (health education and physical therapy, recreation, and physical education) have certain common professional needs.[1] These are pointed out in Chart I. At the top of the

---

[1] As shown by studies of catalogue material; see Chart I.

## Chart I. COMMON AND DIFFERING REQUIREMENTS IN THREE SAMPLE CURRICULA

| Health and Prephysical therapy | Physical education | Recreation leadership |
|---|---|---|

General education common to all: communication skills, mathematics, physical education skills, biological sciences, social sciences including sociology and anthropology, physical sciences, humanities, psychology, history, government

| Health and Prephysical therapy | Physical education | Recreation leadership |
|---|---|---|
| General education: different emphases<br>Zoology, physics, chemistry, bacteriology, genetics | Zoology and sociology | Sociology, economics, anthropology, municipal government |

Preparation for homemaking, common to all: child development, nutrition, home management, problems of marriage and the family, art in the home, human nature and personality, community organization

Professional education common to all: orientation to health, physical education and recreation, physiology, anatomy, kinesiology, basic administrative problems, psychology of adjustment and mental health, first aid, personal and community health

*Different courses in professional education* *

| Health education and prephysical therapy | Physical education | Recreation leadership |
|---|---|---|
| Methods and materials in Health Education<br>School health program<br>Safety education and driver training<br>Home nursing<br>Health examination<br>Correctives (P.E.) *<br>Training program (P.E.) *<br>Hospital recreation (Rec.) *<br>Professional education * (P.E.) * * | Sports<br>Skills of movement exploration<br>Self testing<br>Educational dance<br>Gymnastics<br>School programs for elementary and secondary<br>History and principles of physical education<br>Evaluation<br>Practice teaching<br>Special methods in activities<br>Professional education (H) * *<br>Recreation leadership (R) *<br>Officiating (R) *<br>Recreational dance (R) *<br>Sports management (R) *<br>Group leadership (R) *<br>Public demonstrations (R) *<br>Correctives (H) *<br>Training program (H) * | Fine and applied arts: theatre, crafts, music, graphic and plastic arts<br>Organization of community recreation<br>Social group work<br>City planning<br>History and principles of recreation<br>Field experience in recreation<br>Recreation leadership (P.E.) *<br>Camping and outdoor education (P.E.) *<br>Sports and aquatics (P.E.) *<br>Officiating (P.E.) *<br>Recreational dance (P.E.) *<br>Sports management (P.E.) *<br>Group leadership (P.E.) *<br>Public demonstrations (P.E.) *<br>Hospital recreation (H) * |

* Courses marked with an asterisk will also be needed in the field indicated by initials.

* * Professional education courses vary according to certification requirements in different states, but should be taken by all students preparing to teach.

chart are the customary requirements in general education. Some of these, such as communication skills, physical education skills, and the humanities, are equally stressed in all three lines of preparation. On the other hand, the curriculum preparing for health education and physical therapy emphasizes biological and physical sciences; the curriculum preparing for recreation leadership emphasizes social sciences; while the physical education curriculum has at least one basic course in biology and one in sociology.

Additional study of the chart makes it clear that certain professional courses are found in all three curricula: orientation, physiology, anatomy, kinesiology, general methods, and others. Even the lists of different professional courses show some overlapping between two fields. There is more of this overlapping between physical education and recreation than between health and either of the others. Thus it is obvious that the choice of one of the three lines of specialization need not be made immediately, as the first two years will be very similar, whatever the later specialization.

## Trends in the four-year professional curriculum in physical education

The author examined professional curricula in thirty institutions preparing teachers of physical education. There were several types of schools among them: state universities, teachers colleges, private universities and liberal arts colleges. Geographically they were spread from coast to coast. All save one were coeducational, but in most cases the curricula differed for men and women. Chart II reports on the curricula for women, giving the percentage of this group listing specific course requirements in each of three areas: general education, professional education, and professional physical education.

It may be seen at a glance that there is much greater agreement in the field of physical education than there is in general

Strategy in badminton

The study of Anatomy is basic to all three curricula

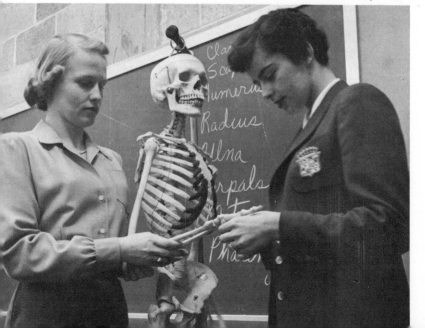

## Chart II. REQUIREMENTS FOR B.A. DEGREE WITH MAJOR IN PHYSICAL EDUCATION

(Women; $N = 30$)

| General Education | | Professional Education | | Professional Physical Education | |
|---|---|---|---|---|---|
| Course | % Requiring | Course | % Requiring | Course | % Requiring |
| Communication (English composition) | 100% | Educational psychology | 70% | Freshman activities | 97% |
| Biological science | 87 | Principles and practices of secondary education | 50 | Sophomore activities | 93 |
| Psychology | 83 | Introduction to education | 47 | Junior activities | 93 |
| Social science | 70 | Child development | 33 | Practice teaching | 93 |
| History | 67 | Methods and principles of teaching | 33 | Physiology | 93 |
| Zoology | 57 | History of education | 13 | Anatomy | 90 |
| Humanities | 57 | Administration of education | 13 | Kinesiology | 87 |
| Speech | 57 | Audiovisual education | 13 | Orientation | 83 |
| Physical science | 43 | Evaluation | 10 | Organization and administration | 83 |
| Sociology | 27 | Guidance | 10 | Special methods (dance and sports) | 83 |
| Government | 27 | Philosophy of education | 10 | Correctives (adaptives) | 80 |
| Chemistry | 23 | Elementary school methods | 10 | Personal and community hygiene | 80 |
| Mathematics | 20 | Social foundations | 10 | Health education | 80 |
| Physics | 17 | Curriculum of education | 7 | History and principles | 73 |
| Foreign language | 13 | School procedure | 7 | First aid | 70 |
| Nutrition | 10 | Adolescent psychology | 7 | Elementary school physical education | 60 |
| | | Educational foundations | 7 | Senior activities | **53** |
| | | Problems in education | 3 | Recreation leadership and community recreation | 50 |
| | | Teacher and child | 3 | Tests and measurements (evaluation) | 50 |
| | | | | Methods (general) | 43 |
| | | | | Physiology of exercise | 40 |
| | | | | Camping | 40 |
| | | | | School hygiene | 27 |
| | | | | High school program | 17 |
| | | | | Safety education | 17 |
| | | | | Analysis of movement | 17 |
| | | | | Recreational crafts | 7 |

NOTE: This chart does not indicate future trends; it merely summarizes present practice.

Electives: Range 4–32 semester hours.
Median 14 semester hours.

education or in professional education. Half or more of the colleges agree on nineteen requirements in physical education, on eight in general education, and on only two in professional education. The lack of agreement on courses in professional education is probably a matter of nomenclature and differing provisions for state certification in different states, rather than failure to accept basic experience in professional education as important to the teacher's preparation. On the other hand, the similarity of requirements in physical education means that the program is well established, that much group study has been given to the needs of teachers in the field, and, perhaps, that the traditional pattern is somewhat rigid. More differences might have been observed if the sport and dance activities required (listed in the chart as freshman activities, sophomore activities, etc.) had been examined in detail. But since this detailed information was given in comparatively few catalogues, it did not seem feasible to report it.

How these requirements are distributed in the four years varies somewhat, but on the whole the practice is to place general education and background sciences in the first two years, leaving the last two for professional courses in education and physical education, health, or recreation. Sample programs, with some preparation for homemaking added as electives, are outlined below. These are not approved by any certification or accrediting groups. In other words, they are not in any sense authoritative.

### SAMPLE PROGRAM FOR WOMEN MAJORING IN PHYSICAL EDUCATION

Freshman Year

| First Semester | Second Semester |
|---|---|
| English (communication) | English |
| Orientation to physical education | Speech |
| Zoology | Zoology |
| Sociology (or general social science) | Sociology, etc. |
| Freshman activities | Freshman activities |

## Sophomore Year

English (literature)
Psychology
Child development
Personal and community health
Sophomore activities

Health education
Recreation leadership
Anatomy
Mental health
Sophomore activities

## Junior Year

Introduction to education
Kinesiology
Physiology
First aid
Art in the home (elective)
Junior activities

Educational psychology
Correctives (adaptives)
Nutrition (elective)
Elementary school physical education
Problems of marriage and the family (elective)
Junior activities

## Senior Year

Practice teaching
History and principles of physical education
Humanities: Fine arts, philosophy, history, etc.
Principles and practice secondary education
Home management (elective)
Senior activities: special methods

Practice teaching
Organization and administration of physical education
Government
Evaluation
Community organization (elective)
Senior activities: special methods

Of course such a sample program is modified in each institution by local requirements outside the specialty, and by local experiments or curricular explorations within the specialty. The electives suggested are all in the homemaking field, and might be varied according to the individual interest of the student.

## SAMPLE PROGRAM FOR WOMEN MAJORS IN HEALTH EDUCATION AND PREPHYSICAL THERAPY COURSE

### Freshman Year

English (communication)
Orientation to health education
Zoology
Chemistry
Freshman activities

English
Speech
Zoology
Chemistry
Personal and community health

### Sophomore Year

| | |
|---|---|
| Social Science | Social Science |
| Psychology | Mental health |
| Child development | Anatomy |
| Physiology | Nutrition |
| Sophomore activities | First aid |
| | Sophomore activities |

### Junior Year

| | |
|---|---|
| Introduction to education | Educational psychology |
| Kinesiology | Correctives (adaptives) |
| Bacteriology | Public health |
| Safety education and driver training | School health programs |
| Government | History |
| Physics | Physics |

### Senior Year

| | |
|---|---|
| Practice teaching or field work in community health | Practice teaching or field work |
| Home nursing (elective) | Health inspection and examination |
| Hospital recreation | Home management (elective) |
| Humanities: Fine arts, philosophy | Problems of marriage and family (elective) |
| Principles and practice of secondary education | Audiovisual aids (elective) |
| Methods and materials of health education | Art in the home (elective) |

Since there seems to be less agreement among different institutions giving majors in health education and recreation than there is in the physical education major, these may be less "typical" courses than the first one described. For some years to come, there will be a great deal of variation in programs of individual institutions offering these three majors. At the same time, groups of colleges, as well as professional organizations, will continue to study problems of curriculum and to make suggestions that carry out results of their studies.

The physical education activities listed for the first two years generally include self-testing, swimming, creative dance, movement exploration, body mechanics, and posture training, with some individual sports such as archery and bowling.

Women's Recreation Association Cabin

## SAMPLE PROGRAM FOR WOMEN MAJORS IN
## RECREATION LEADERSHIP

### Freshman Year

English (communication)
Orientation to recreation
Biological science
Sociology
Freshman activities

English
Speech
Biological science
Sociology
Freshman activities

### Sophomore Year

English (literature)
Psychology
Child development
Camping and outdoor education
Physiology
Sophomore activities

Recreation leadership
Mental health
Anatomy
Recreational crafts
Nutrition
Sophomore activities

### Junior Year

Kinesiology
Field work in recreation
Applied arts: music, drama, etc.
Community organization
Junior activities

Economics
Field work in recreation
Applied arts
Municipal government
Junior activities

Senior Year

| Principles and methods of recreation | Organization and administration of recreation |
| Problems of marriage and family (elective) | Field work in recreation |
| Anthropolgy | Human nature and personality |
| Social group work | Government |
| First aid and safety education | Hospital recreation |
| Art in the home (elective) | Home management (elective) |

The recreation major's activity preparation will tend toward sports and recreational dance, with, perhaps some work in posture, movement exploration, and fitness programs which are popular in Y.W.C.A. situations.

None of these programs are represented as "ideal"—they do, however, show general trends. The electives in homemaking are not chosen as often as might be inferred; but, the content of Chapter 3 points strongly to the importance of these courses for all women. The freshman must remember, moreover, that no blueprint will fit all schools, because the objectives of various colleges will differ, and their programs will differ accordingly.

### Extracurricular experiences

College graduates look back with nostalgic pleasure on what they learned outside the classroom. Managing the swim show or the dance program was an "education in itself," they often say. They will tell the undergraduate that exploring the library or joining some academic interest club may open doors to other worlds of information and ideas. Social contacts in living groups teach acceptance of persons with different backgrounds, and understanding of the influence of those backgrounds. Talking over common problems, like and unlike interests, opinions, human motives, ideas, and standards helps in the lifelong effort to understand people. Meeting dozens of young men and women, knowing them casually, then exploring the possibilities of stronger ties of court-ship, or friendship with those who seem most appealing, fosters patterns of human relationship that have permanent influence. Most alumnae and upper classmen agree that contacts with others in clubs or organizations with definite projects gives much valuable information about both men and women friends. Their contacts tell if they are responsible, "good troupers" in a pinch, resourceful in emergencies, fun to be with at any time, considerate and ready to recognize the contributions of others. Such qualities may not appear on the surface in everyday situations, but it is important to discover them, since they do give durability to friendship.

Another valuable experience is to share in a first-class extra-curricular production. Whether this is a public program, a publication, a sportsday, or a match game; if it is good enough to give great satisfaction to the participants, it may point up the drive to excellence. To achieve excellence takes self-discipline, drudgery, and pushing one's powers to the limit. It is to be hoped that students can get this satisfaction in much of their course work,[2] however, the extracurricular project often demands responsibility, ingenuity, and close team work "beyond the line of duty" as the saying goes. Thus the informal education to be found on the college campus is not to be discounted, although there is no doubt that some students need to deemphasize it in their own lives. Individual problems and interests in extracurricular activities will be discussed in the next chapter.

## Graduate program

If a freshman's goal is to teach health or physical education in a college situation she will have to have one or more years of graduate study to qualify for such a position. Physical

---

[2] See Chap. 5.

**Men enjoy the skill and power they develop in Modern Dance**

therapy preparation also takes a year beyond the bachelor's degree; in this case it is a good idea to take the specialized graduate training immediately after receiving the B.A. degree. However, those preparing for teaching are usually advised to get two or three years of experience, preferably in public schools, before going on to the M.A. degree. There are several good reasons for this advice. Experience makes graduate courses more meaningful, and makes the graduate student

more ready to participate in graduate seminars and research conferences with other mature students and teachers. For another thing, the experienced graduate student is usually more definite in her choice of areas of specialization, and of problems she wishes to investigate. Then there is another very practical consideration: if the M.A. program is to be preparation for a career, it will in all probability lead to teaching in a major department; for this, public school experience is essential. The author has known many young college teachers who have found this gap in their experience to be a handicap. Some of them go from college teaching to high-school teaching and make the transition without too much trouble. However, most of them recognize that it is easier to go up the age scale than down as they become more mature teachers. That is why most institutions consider experience as well as undergraduate record in awarding graduate assistantships.

## Number and location of professional training courses

The United States Office of Education published, in 1954, a study of institutions offering professional preparation in the three fields of health, physical education, and recreation.[3] Table V has been compiled by the author from their findings.

Table V.  PROFESSIONAL CURRICULA FOR WOMEN IN HEALTH, PHYSICAL EDUCATION AND RECREATION

|  | Total | Health and Physical Education | Physical Education | Health | Recreation | Recreation Combinations |
|---|---|---|---|---|---|---|
| Number of institutions | 635[a] | 280 | 218 | 57 | 77 | 21 |
| Number of states represented | 48[b] | 42 | 48[b] | 25 | 30 | 17 |

[a] Since some institutions offered separate programs in two areas, the total cannot be derived from this table. It is given elsewhere in the report.
[b] Including Alaska—none reported in Rhode Island.

The largest group (289) offer combined courses in health and physical education; they are located in 42 different states. The next largest group (218) offer courses in physical educa-

---

[3] *Undergraduate and Graduate Professional Preparation in Health Education, Physical Education, and Recreation* (Washington, U.S. Department of Health, Education, and Welfare, 1954).

tion only; they are located in 48 different states. Recreation courses *per se* were reported by 77 schools in 30 states, and 21 schools in 17 states offered various combined programs with recreation.[4] Obviously any student wishing professional education in any of these three fields may find it fairly close to home.

## Selecting the school

Most of the readers of this text have already selected the institution in which they are receiving professional preparation. However those who are in Junior colleges or still in high school may be able to use suggestions on the selection of one among the 635 institutions offering one or more programs in health, physical education, or recreation. Included in this number are widely diverse types: women's colleges and coeducational institutions; state universities and small privately supported colleges; teachers' colleges and liberal arts colleges. Within each type the professional programs and other educational experiences available will differ in quality. There is no accreditation system by which schools in this field are graded, as medical schools are graded by the American Medical Association.[5] The candidate must work at getting factual information that will help her to choose wisely.

She may secure information and opinions from many sources, and she needs to consider many factors in making her choice. First, perhaps, she needs to take a look at her own needs and goals. Has she any clear cut wish to specialize in any one area such as teaching health, teaching sports, teaching dance,

---

[4] With both health and physical education in ten schools, with physical education in four schools, as recreation therapy in two, with religious education, elementary education, with camping and Christian education, as recreation administration, and with social studies—one each of the last five programs.

[5] However, accreditation by such various agencies as the North Central and the National Council for Accreditation of Teacher Education may be found in the College Blue Book, published annually.

or playground work? Not all schools are equally qualified in all areas. In corresponding with schools it would be well to find out what faculty member is in charge of the particular specialization, what her training and experience has been, and whether she has written any articles the prospective student might read. Next, does the student want to be on a coeducational campus, or would she prefer to do most of her dating at weekends? A woman's college may be a very lively social spot from Friday to Monday, but during the week there is said to be more time for work than there is if dating is a daily pursuit. Is the student the right temperament for a large institution: is she self-reliant, looking forward to the opportunities of meeting many persons of her own age, and the varied advantages of large libraries, well-equipped laboratories, lectures, plays, concerts, and a wealth of other cultural offerings? Is she ready to compete with many others for grades, sorority membership, honors, and a place in the sun of campus organization? Or does she find this sort of thing distasteful, and prefer the more sheltered, more intimate, more homelike relations of a small school? What about location? Is there any region of the United States which she has long been curious to see? Does she want to get away from home and to be on her own, or does she want to come back for weekends and keep up with home ties?

Second, what are the family's wishes? What financial limitations are there? Of course one's own state or municipal university probably has the lowest fees, and it offers the additional advantage of low travel costs, of a congenial group of friends and neighbors on the campus, or in local alumnae groups after graduation. Does either parent have a definite opinion about the best school for the daughter? Is there a family tradition to be considered? Does the family put a premium on close-to-home location? Do they have prejudices that may need to be dispelled by visits to the campus? When the wishes of parents and daughter are in conflict it may be difficult to find an acceptable compromise. If the parents provide the money it is reasonable to think that they will want to determine if it is being wisely invested. On the other hand, the college years are to be lived by the daughter, not by the parents. Her experiences there will be part of her equipment for work and other aspects of her life. If both parents and daughter can select the school by closely reasoned investigation rather than by rumor, propaganda, and slanted information, there'll be better satisfaction with the result.

A third source of information is the advice of guidance personnel. Advisers know various sources of information, can help with interpreting college catalogues, can estimate the students' chances for admission and for academic success in college. Students of high ability may get some pressure from advisers to go into science and mathematics, which are now receiving national emphasis, or some field other than physical education or recreation. The need for academic competence in our area is not very well understood, and so may be underemphasized by teachers of other subjects. Teachers of physical education, on the other hand, know that this need has been repeatedly demonstrated, and they will usually encourage their students' choice of their own specialization. Usually teachers will promote attendance at their own schools, and this is to be expected. If different teachers of physical education are asked to give the names of the top ten schools training teachers in the field, and if several agree on certain schools, regardless of their own affiliation, this may be considered a very favorable recommendation.

Fourth, various communications from the colleges themselves give many useful facts. When reading a college catalogue it is well to note the stated purposes of the department, the course requirements, the possibilities for general education and for electives, the number of faculty members and their qualifications, and the facilities for sports and for housing. Admission requirements, costs of tuition, board, and room, and programs of student aid, are usually described in other parts of the

catalogue. After study of the catalogue, some questions may
need to be asked by correspondence. In this case it is advisable
to write directly to the head of the department of physical education for women, or to the departmental adviser to women
major students. If such a letter is answered carefully and in
helpful detail, this fact in itself gives evidence that the department treats students with consideration as individuals, not
merely as statistics. Often interviews with field representatives
give the chance to ask questions about college life behind the
scenes. For instance, what is the sorority-fraternity situation?
Do independents have a chance in extracurricular activities?
How long is the rushing period? What are the extra costs of
sorority membership? What housing does the college offer?
How large are the housing units? How is student government
organized? What regulations and supervision control student
social life? What is the student body like? How much difference
in background? What percentage are working for part or all of
their expenses? What cultural advantages are offered by the
college or the city? What is the denomination of the college,
and the religious participation of the students? Is there a church
of our denomination in the city? What provision is there for
student-faculty contacts? Who are the outstanding faculty members on the campus? The best answers to these and to unspoken
questions about the quality of guidance available to students,
may be found on visits to the campus. On these visits both the
prospective student and the parent will want to talk with faculty
members and with other students in the daughter's field. They
will want to ask where last year's graduates are placed, and
whether incoming freshman majors have a departmental adviser who has time for conferences as needed. They will want
to meet this adviser: the daughter will be asking herself if she
could approach this woman with her personal problems; the
mother will be asking herself if this is the kind of person she'd
like to have counseling her daughter. The daughter will need
some time with students when no grown-ups are about; the

mother will want to talk at her own level with other adults when no students are present. The visit to the campus may well be the last step in making the big decision. The steps described are, perhaps, laborious but it is better to be self-directing in this important process than to be like a billiard ball—just rolled into some pocket by an outside force.

## QUESTIONS

1. Are you getting the values you should from general education courses? Should these come early or late in one's college years? Why?

2. What does it mean to "live freely and productively in our society?" Is this possible for persons in the United States who have not been to college? For college graduates in the U.S.S.R.? In England? In Germany? In India? In Ghana?

3. Are you surprised at the number of colleges and universities giving professional education in physical education, health education, recreation, and prephysical therapy? Do you expect this number to increase or decrease in the next ten years? Why?

4. If you were advising the girl next door would you suggest a large university or a small college? Why?

5. What did you yourself get out of direct communication with this or other colleges?

## SELECTED REFERENCES

AAHPER. *Professional Preparation of Recreation Personnel* (Washington: AAHPER, 1957), pp. 19–27.

Fraley, Lester, Warren Johnson, and Benjamin Murray, ed. *Physical Education and Healthful Living* (Englewood Cliffs: Prentice-Hall, 1954), pp. 3–38.

Jenny, John H. *Introduction to Recreation Education* (Philadelphia: Saunders, 1955), Appendix B.

Johnson, Granville, Warren Johnson, and James Humphrey. *Your Career in Physical Education* (New York: Harper, 1957), Chap. IX.

Knapp, Clyde, and Ann E. Jewett. *Physical Education Student and Beginning Teacher* (New York: McGraw-Hill, 1957), Chap. II.

National Recreation Association. *How to Choose the Right College for Your Career in Recreation* (New York: NRA, 1954).

Smith, Julian. *Outdoor Education for American Youth* (Washington: AAHPER, 1957), Chap. IV.

Snyder, R. A., and H. A. Scott. *Professional Preparation in Health, Physical Education and Recreation* (New York: McGraw-Hill, 1954), Chap. 3.

*The National Conference on Undergraduate Professional Preparation in Physical Education, Health Education, and Recreation* (Chicago: The Athletic Institute, 1948), Chap. 2, 3, 4, 5, 6, 7, 8, 9.

CHAPTER **5**

*Professional Preparation:*

## INDIVIDUAL PROBLEMS

IN THE LAST chapter we reported surveys which
show the general trends in professional preparation for careers
in teaching health and physical education as well as in recreation leadership. This chapter purports to discuss certain individual problems with the reader and to assist you in thinking
through and working through your own problems.

### Understanding your own curriculum

Do you know what courses you'll be taking next semester?
How they fit with those you are taking now? Does your program
make sense to you? What about the courses you are in now?
It might be a first step in understanding to try to get at the
point, or the *raison d'etre* as the French say, of each course.
Why does the University require you to take English composi-
tion (or communication skills)? What is the instructor driving
at? Where does that leave you; i.e., do you have any goal except to get the best possible grade and finish off one troublesome
requirement? Let's try analyzing these three sets of goals for

freshman English: the University's, the instructor's and yours. The University wants its graduates to be able to write and speak like educated men and women. On the job, in the home, in the community, they should be understood; that is, they should express to others their ideas and their feelings clearly and effectively. The instructor wants his students to write correctly, sloughing off the errors of careless habits formed earlier. Of course your instructor has personal goals: developing his ability to interest his classes, getting response from them, watching them improve, working at his own research or creative writing; in a word, building his own successful career. Remember, he has not chosen teaching as an easy or highly profitable way of life. Think over the things that might be rewarding to him and see what you can do about them. Your own goals are essential: will writing and speaking effectively be useful to you? In college? In your career? These are rhetorical questions, for you very well know the answers. In college you'll be writing term reports, essay type examinations, how-to-do-it explanations. You'll be speaking at assemblies, in class discussions, at organization meetings and in "yak" sessions. As a teacher, you'll be explaining and talking purposefully to your students. By careful analysis and your own hard work, the three lines of purposes may merge into one:

University—the educated alumna   ⎫ Students' habitual
Instructor—the responsive-improving class ⎪ competence in
   Student—greatest possible improvement ⎰ writing and
          through instruction, study and ⎱ speaking
          practice


Without such analysis and effort they may remain separate:

University—the educated alumna
Instructor—the responsive class
   Student—getting a grade and "finishing" a requirement

Try this plan on zoology, sociology or swimming. Perhaps it is more difficult to see what history or philosophy may mean to you. Mrs. Mueller has well said that liberal arts courses and general education should be stressed in the education of modern woman: [1]

> For a woman needs an independent spirit much more than an independent income. To offset the economic handicap and to cope with her changing roles, she needs an inner stability and poise which come not from skills but from knowledge and understanding. Since she is still expected to take the lead in cultural activities and in developing the happiness and welfare of her children, she must know the fine as well as the culinary arts. . . .
>
> . . . Liberal education is an attitude of mind and spirit; it is knowledge that is touched with beauty, not the easy reverence which is devoid of understanding. It is also knowledge fused with emotion, changing mere tolerance and openmindedness into conviction and confidence, and sometimes into action. It eschews an insipid peace of mind, looks for the challenge, welcomes the crisis. It pursues the meanings behind the appearances, and invokes the dynamics of the thinking process rather than the static properties of truth.

In a sophomore ethics class one acquaintance of the author's remembered a statement heard as a student which served as a guide to problems the rest of her life. This was the so-called Ethical Imperative stated centuries ago by Immanuel Kant, a German philosopher:

> So act as to treat humanity, in yourself or others, as an end always, never as a means only.

It has been described as a down-to-earth application of the Christian ideal of the brotherhood of man and the Golden Rule. A freshman who believed in it and lived it could not be

---

[1] Kate Hevner Mueller, *Educating Women for a Changing World* (Minneapolis: University of Minnesota Press, 1954), pp. 283–85. By permission.

an apple-polisher, could not "stand up" one date if a better one came along later. You may spell out many other applications of the ethical imperative to problems of human relations. To the student who listens, reads, thinks, and remembers, other and similarly illuminating ideas may continue to come from her college courses.

## Success in study and course work

Of course, every student would like to be successful, but not very many define success realistically. In the diagram on the previous page we have suggested as a goal the "greatest possible improvement through instruction, study, and practice." In other words, driving toward excellence. How can a student of *B* or *C* capacity do excellent work? She can't hope to excel the *A* students in her class. This is where realistic appraisal comes in. If the student concentrates on excelling her own record, on stretching her ability to the very best of her capacity, she will be achieving success in terms of her individual equipment, even if she gets a *C* grade in the course. On the other hand, if she has top capacity and doesn't stretch her ability to the very best of her capacity, she is *not* successful although her grade may be *B*.

Let's analyze this stretching process as it applies to instruction, study, and practice. There are techniques which cut down waste motion and make effort more effective in each of these phases. Getting the most out of instruction means coming to class with an objective attitude: leaving emotions at the door. Neither resenting the instructor nor effusively admiring him, the objective student listens closely to what he is saying, takes useful notes, thinks, and relates the lecture material of the day to the rest of the course content. In discussion groups, she listens, respects other students' contributions, makes her own if pertinent, and learns to summarize in her notes the gist of common agreement or conclusions of the discussion. She asks questions and learns to participate without monopolizing group time. Her notes are clear, readable, and not in stenographic shorthand.

Study is largely a matter of concentrating and organizing, as you may have discovered. To concentrate you must have a clear idea of the assignment (which you have written down in class) and plan a way to get it done. Then you get at it immediately: no fiddling about sharpening pencils, looking for notebooks, texts or dictionary, which should be in their customary places close to your study desk. The first reading of the assignment should be a quick look for the main ideas of the chapter which are jotted down in your notebook as topic headings in a skeleton outline. The second more careful reading fills in material related to the topic headings and yields pertinent questions for additional reading or class discussion. Unfamiliar words should be looked up during reading. If the textbook is your own copy, underlining main topics is not a bad idea, but it makes the book unfit for use by others. During the second reading, you should be alert for these things:

a. Facts: names, dates in social science; structures, functions, life processes and experimental evidence in biological science, with the authority (if no footnote is given it may be assumed that the author of the text is the authority: his name and academic background should be learned).

b. Relationships: causes, results, comparisons (both likenesses and differences), relationships in time and place.

c. Principles: general truths based on a number of related facts.

d. Use of principles: applying them to new situations or unfamiliar problems.

The second reading yields an outline with main divisions, subheads, facts, ideas and principles in a pattern of relationship.

This is the basic organization of material, and the plan of organization makes understanding and remembering possible. Class notes and study notes supplement each other, and should be kept in the same division of the looseleaf notebook. Each day before class new material should be reviewed briefly and at the end of the week a more thorough review of the week's work should be made.

Practice is evaluating and using what you are learning as well as preparing for tests. In a foreign language, for example Spanish, evaluation takes you back to the goal of the course; we could call it making you a more competent citizen by understanding better our Latin American neighbors. If you are taking spoken Spanish, you will note the formalities and courtesies of greetings and inquiries; you'll be struck with a certain built-in vagueness in expressing time: *mañana;* these differences you learn to accept as part of their life-pattern without irritation or contempt. As you listen to a cultivated voice speaking the language (on a record, over television, or in class work), you'll be impressed with the beauty of diction and inflection and will try to imitate it. Teaming up with a classmate for this practice will make your speaking more effective, and listening to a tape recording of your own efforts will give you an idea of errors to be corrected. If you go to International Club and meet students from Latin America, it will be a real adventure to try even your first few phrases on them. Such practice, reenforced by review of class work and text, concentrated hard study of vocabulary and grammar, and writing sentences you want to speak, will take you up to tests and examinations without panic. In a similar way, practice of tennis backhand and forehand strokes against a backboard (or with a ball throwing machine), studying your "how-to-do-it" text and tennis rules, playing the game with classmates of your own ability level, and your dates who are probably better than you are; all this reenforces your classtime instruction. Again, when tests come at the end of the term you are ready for them with a brief review of class notes and text or rule book.

Writing an essay type examination involves a careful reading of the question, recalling and organizing pertinent material, writing it in clear, short but related sentences in legible handwriting. The question tells you what is called for in the first verb:

*Discuss:* state the problem and present various aspects, points of view, efforts to solve it.

*List:* simply enumerate, briefly but clearly, without discussing.

*Compare:* give the similarities and differences of the topic in question.

Many other verbs may be used.[2]

In an essay examination, divide and watch your time. If there are three questions to be answered in a 60-minute period and you know much more about #2 than either of the others, you might well go to work on a 15–30–15-minute basis rather than a 20–20–20. However, don't forget that the last fifteen minutes is to be given entirely to the last question.

Objective tests call for careful reading, first of directions for the entire test, then for each part as you answer it—not for each item, since directions for Part II will apply to every one of the 20–30– or 50 items in Part II. Then read carefully and be sure you understand the meaning of each separate item before answering it. Go through the entire test, answering first the questions you are reasonably certain of (most authorities advise leaving these answers unchanged). Then come back to the unanswered items, analyzing the question as best you can and thinking of the reasons for your answer. Before turning in

[2] John R. Chandler, G. C. Beamer, C. C. Williams, and V. L. Armstrong, *Successful Adjustment in College* (Englewood Cliffs: Prentice-Hall, 1951), p. 50.

your paper, check your understanding of the directions for each part.

Preparing for examinations, as has been said, may best be done by daily study and weekly review. A final review on the day before the test will be very helpful if done at a reasonable hour, leaving enough time for sleep. In the author's opinion studying with other students is usually a waste of time because it often means sharing fears rather than information. However, if you find a group that really stimulates independent thinking through discussion this is good. If there remain points you do not understand note them down for class questions, or ask for a conference with your instructor. If several of you have the same problems to clear up, it will save your instructor's time if you ask for a group conference with him or with one of his assistants.

Evaluating your own progress should be helped by knowing your grade on a written assignment or an examination. The grade, of course, is your instructor's evaluation of your performance on the paper or test. This may be hard to take. If you have gone through this "stretching" process of hard work and know that your skills and understandings have increased, it will be a severe blow to be graded C or less. You may respond in one or more of several ways, according to your temperament:

1. Tears, resentment against the instructor, a feeling of injustice, unfairness, anguished and very verbal complaints.
2. Hidden disappointment, bewilderment, deep discouragement, and a "what's the use" attitude of despondency.
3. Rehash of the test with your classmates, who may or may not remember their answers, and may or may not be satisfied with their grades. Usually there's not much help or comfort in this process.

4. After the necessary "cooling off" period, an effort to clear up your own errors and to list the areas where you need more work toward a better understanding.

5. An evaluation of your study habits.

A word of advice: don't go near your instructor if you are in the first three stages of shock! If you can readily get help from him in stage 4, do so. Your approach, obviously, is never, "Why did *you* give *me* such a low grade?" It should be, "What do *I* need to do for a better understanding of this material?" (or to improve my skills or my memory of important facts). Probably you have a class adviser who may have more time to help you and a better understanding of your needs than the instructor. If so, see her first.

A word may be in order here about apple-polishing or the devious pursuit of grades for the sake of grades by fair means or foul. Remember Kant's Ethical Imperative: "So act as to treat humanity, in yourself or others, as an end always, never as a means only." Apple polishing is far out of line with this dictum. Not only are you *using* your instructor's human weakness for flattery or for the appeal of a pretty girl, as a means to a better grade, but you are being unfair to yourself! You are *using* your own charm, your particular brand of humanity, as a *means* to a grade, forgetting your more important objective or end: to learn something from the course. Then there is a practical objection to apple polishing: you label yourself as an insincere person; your adviser, other faculty members and students know you as such, and it does your record no good— no good at all. A major department is a college version of one's own family, small enough so you know each other's strengths and weaknesses. Remember, "flattery gets you nowhere." Whatever your first crop of grades, keep on pushing toward your own standard of excellence, and keep on using the course material you have mastered so that it becomes your own.

## The college library

This building should know you well, and you should know it better. After your first few weeks on the campus, you have formed at least a nodding acquaintance (not to be confused with nodding for physiological reasons) with the library. This may be limited to a mannerly approach to the reserve desk to secure an elusive required reference, a retreat to the nearest reading table, followed by operation concentration which holds at bay your more sociably inclined friends. As the weeks go on, you'll need to explore the other resources of the library since you are expected to do independent investigation. The card catalogue—by subject, or author, or title—will begin to make sense; the *Readers Guide to Periodical Literature* will help you find current articles on any given subject; the *Book Review*

An open-shelf library is best for study and for browsing

*State University of Iowa*

*Digest* gives excerpts of reviews of books, arranged by authors, with an index of subjects at the end. You soon learn the library's ground rules for finding and using books in the library, and taking out the books you'd like to study elsewhere; don't hesitate to ask questions about these rules. Be ready, also, to ask the reference librarian for help in locating material on any subject you are studying. If study in the main reading room is difficult because of interruptions, find a hideout. This could be in the stacks, if open to freshmen. It could be in a secluded spot around the corner, behind newspaper racks, or even in an adjacent empty classroom (if any). The books you have found should be examined by a brief look at the author, his position, the date of publication and references in the index to the subject you are investigating; this is followed by a more careful reading and note-taking of material. Notes should be placed on small cards, each card identified by the name of the author; at least one of each set having complete documentation as follows:

Murray, Ruth L.: *Dance in Education* (New York: Harper, 1953), pp. 25–29

Material should be paged as you read it, since your footnotes will need to give the page reference. Any borrowed idea should be footnoted, even if you do not use the author's exact words; any word-for-word quotation should be enclosed in quotation marks and footnoted as well. This should be done *as you read,* since your time is far too valuable to be used in retracing your study steps and hunting for forgotten sources.

## Building your own library

Buy your text books and keep them; be sure they are the latest editions because the chapter and page references differ in different editions and because the author has made improvements in later editions. The edition may be identified on the title page and should be checked whether you are buying a new or secondhand book. In the latter case, examine the book to see if it is in good shape: not underlined (this interferes with your own ideas in reading) nor with marginal notes; not mutilated by having pages or pictures cut out of it; not "coming apart at the seams" nor dirty with use. In short, a new book is by far the best buy, just as a new car is better than a used one. Ask your family to give you a book plate for a birthday or Christmas present, and be sure each of your books is so labeled. Supplement your text book library with useful references: a student dictionary, a book of synonyms, rules of correct English usage, the latest rule books in different sports (since rules change); any references, fiction, or (general) contemporary books of interest you like especially. Your personal library is the foundation for the home library which will build up as your own family grows. To have well-read, well-loved books around you is like having good friends with you always. These good friends know more than you do, have traveled more widely, have experienced more than your life can encompass, but they never patronize you nor assume airs of superiority. They are "at your service" in a very real sense, whether giving help in professional problems, in human relationships, in understanding your world, in sharing an unforgettable human document, or just providing a companionable and entertaining evening.

### Study, reading, browsing

College experience is rich if it gives you these three habits or skills, or pleasures—whatever you want to call them. If you can read closely, organizing, thinking, and remembering as you go, you can study. If you read quickly, accurately, questioningly and widely, you may share experience with gifted minds of all ages and places. If you love to browse in any library, thumbing through new books or old, you have an antidote for boredom. If you learn to read aloud to others of like tastes, you are discovering a form of inexpensive recreation that yields priceless returns to any family or to any other group.

## Success in skills

A junior major, usually a cheerful, charmingly gay young person, came into the author's office many years ago in anything but a gay or cheerful mood. She was discouraged about her skill in sports and was convinced that she was not good enough as a performer to be able to teach physical education. As we talked, it became obvious that she was evaluating herself on the basis of her grades in activities, not on her success as a leader of groups on the playground. This she enjoyed and did very well, as she finally admitted. We talked a good deal that day about skill in teaching as compared with skill in performance, and it became clear that these were two different things. In some individuals these skills went together and strengthened each other; in others they did not. We also talked about other attributes of teaching: understanding children and even adolescents, and getting along with them. Finally the student's discouragement lifted a little, and she decided to think over her problem more carefully. She did graduate in physical education and had a spectacularly successful career as a teacher, recreation leader, and later as a recreation administrator. Marriage and a family interrupted, but did not end her career. Many other examples come to mind: highly skilled performers who are poor teachers because they start beginners with the most complex and advanced details; highly skilled performers who remember progression, sense the class's level of development and take them along easily; average performers who are excellent teachers, and so on.

Naturally each freshman major will want to become skilled in every activity! Earlier in this chapter, ways of practicing tennis skills were mentioned. The same method may be used in any sport or dance form. Then comes the question: should I

### Water ballet

have fun becoming tops in my best sport, or should I try to get better in the things I don't do well? When a superb golfer (runner-up in the state tournament during senior year in high school) started her four-year major in physical education, she decided to catch up on all the other sports and forget golf until summer. This she did her first two years, had fun and did well in everything else—except field hockey. In her junior year she was elected president of the women's recreation association's golf club, and did a fine promotional job in that capacity. On graduation she taught golf and other sports in a junior college until she married. After marriage she took up tournament golf again, finally won the state championship and achieved national ranking.

Setting goals and a program of extra class practice in activity performance is a problem for the individual major to talk over with her adviser. She should remember, however, that she'll be expected to teach various forms of physical education when she graduates, and that the four-year major program in activities is designed to provide for adequate proficiency as a teacher in all of them. On the other hand, some specialization as an undergraduate will give her fun as well as a basis for specialization later in her teaching career, and a resource for her own adult recreation.

## Extracurricular experience

In the last chapter we talked about some of the general values college women have found in experience outside class. Your own extracurricular work and play will be a response to your own problems. Economic necessity may have to come first: if you are earning a large part of your expenses, your job provides the means of a college education, and so makes demands on a definite part of your time. After the first year you may be able to secure a job that causes the least possible disruption to the schedule: dormitory board jobs have this advantage. Board and room jobs with a family are good in many ways, but you need to make sure that your baby-sitting time is a definite part of your paid work, and that a regular afternoon or evening time is scheduled for your favorite club.

You may have certain curricular needs: extra quiz sections or remedial work in reading if your progress is less than average, or interest clubs if you are good enough to make them. These may be along academic lines: French club, chamber music groups, writing workshops, debate society, science, home economics, or craft clubs. They may be in activities: clubs in various sports or dance, or the women's recreation association which is influential on almost every campus. Your departmental major club is, of course, a must. Here, as well as in many of your classes and women's recreation association clubs, you'll meet some of the men specializing in physical education. They have many interests similar to yours, and will be fun to know. It will be good also to know your instructors and advisers

### Horse show of riding club

in an informal setting. The professional meetings of your major club may open new avenues of interest, new career possibilities, and add to the reasons why you are proud of your choice of a profession.

Your residence group, be it dormitory or sorority, will exert pressures on you for extra-curricular participation. It is wise to go along with these *in moderation*. Be warned, however, that a point system, if used by sororities to develop latent talents among shy or indifferent members, is not to be taken as a goal for the active, vigorous freshman of many interests. Collecting points will be easy, but it may defeat your main purposes in college by scattering your efforts.

As an individual, you may have personality needs that affect extra-curricular participation. The chances are that you are more of an extrovert than introvert,[3] but if you happen to be one of the "shy ones," don't force yourself into many groups your first year. Select one group along the lines of your best ability, and work hard within this group volunteering for any job that needs to be done. Gradually increase your circle of acquaintances, in classes, in clubs, in your housing situation. Help any second semester freshmen or other persons who appear to need a little "know how." Be sure to start some volunteer community work before your senior year, so the adjustment to practice teaching or field work will be more readily made. On the other hand, if you are one of the hardy extroverts, you'll have to use self-discipline. Don't branch out into every group that appeals to you; don't make a best friend and confidant of every person who sits next to you in class or every boy who asks for a date. Be selective.

The advantages of sharing in an excellent, highly successful extracurricular project are very great, as we have stated in the previous chapter. In the early stages of such a project, the dif-

---

[3] See Chap. 2, p. 49.

## Harmonica Hoedown

ference between a mediocre and excellent result is established by the responsibility of the students concerned. This is where any group member can push by putting on group pressure for getting things done on time; soon the production will start rolling and develop its own momentum. Watch the pace of the group and the project. If you naturally work slowly and accurately, the project momentum may get beyond you, the due dates begin to pile up, and then frustration piles up, also. Then you will have to learn to look for help and organize help by delegating responsibility. The work will not be done as well as if you did it all (perhaps), but the team work of the project will be better, and you may learn how to adjust to different rates of work. In addition, you may save yourself from becoming a perfectionist.

## Community service

In a sense, all your extra-curricular activities are community service. However, it is good to look beyond the college walls to the needs of the town. At least two avenues are open to this extramural work: practice teaching or fieldwork, and work in your own church. If your practice teaching is to be as valuable as it should be, you'll want to know individual children: first in your class, then through the eyes of their home room teacher, then in their family, neighborhood and community situation.[4] Work with Scouts or other youth groups is of great help in understanding adolescents. The Y.W.C.A. also is always look- for volunteers who enjoy older groups. Your church is eager to serve, and in turn to be served by college students. At first, church attendance may be just a satisfying continuation of your established Sunday pattern of worship, at home. Then the youth discussion-groups in the church may attract you. Sooner or later, if you are thinking closely about religion in your life, you will want to give some of your time and strength in return for the privileges of worship and religious education that the church has given you. Whatever channel your effort finds, religion will then become a living part of you, and you will become more than a weekly observer of the service.

---

[4] Space does not permit describing details of the process by which you come to know children in this way. Your methods teachers and supervisors of practice teaching will help you to do this.

*Wayne State University*

### Brave Cowboy Bill

### *Schedules*

Time for all this: serious study, practice of skills, extracurricular projects, sleep and community service will be yours only if you organize your schedule. Perhaps you have tried this without success. Something special is always interfering—you don't want to miss getting acquainted with a new date, or an argument starts after class: you get involved and don't want to walk out; someone comes in your room just when you get settled for study: the "short" bridge session turns into an evening of cards; there's always a special concert, lecture, meeting, or emergency exam which you have not anticipated, so the schedule "blows up" and seems wrecked beyond repair.

Scheduling during the first year of college is a great help if you learn to make it serve you, and if you accept the fact that flexible rearrangement is a part of the process. It can serve you by making use of those empty single hours between classes if you put down the best place as well as the best time for your study. As you come out of your English class at 10:00, with nothing on your schedule until zoology at 11:00, you must decide whether to go to the dorm for the mail, to the union for a coffee break, to the library to study something or other, or just to sit on the steps in the sun with Chuck, who has suddenly discovered his interest in you. Now the purpose of your schedule is not to save you from the clutches of the coffee break habit, or from Chuck; it is, rather, to save you from frustration —with yourself and with all the undone chores that pile up if you try to work only when there's nothing else to do. In a word, the schedule is the framework of organized effort, and only organized effort will take you where you want to go.

Flexible rearrangement of the schedule is important. Work with it for two weeks, as closely as you can, then revise it where the weak parts show and try it again. Realize that if it is knocked to pieces this week, it can be mended next week by a little rearrangement. Soon you'll be getting some real insights into your own needs and possibilities, and will find it possible to relax as you are getting the upperhand in your job of college work.

### Adjusting to all age groups

To yourself you are still wondering what Chuck will think when you walk off with your schedule instead of staying to talk with him. What will your roommate say when you hang up a DO NOT DISTURB sign on the door, or if you are always in the library when you are not at meals or asleep? In other words, if you are too concerned with your schedule, won't you lose friends and influence no one? This is possible, of course, if you make your schedule a conversation piece. But if you keep it as your own business and think up ways of easing off into the next spot you should be in, instead of marching off in a self-righteous busy-busy mood, you won't hurt anyone—least of all yourself. For instance, you might say to Chuck, "Come on, walk me over to zoology lab." Then at that building simply say, "Bye now—see you," or whatever coin your vocabulary furnishes for a friendly farewell. No excuse, not a word about the schedule or what you are going to do; elusive mystery perhaps, but it will do your cause no harm.

Adjusting to your own age group is not too hard. This can be done at either of two levels: the surface level of using charm techniques which you can find in a dozen books and which you come to discount in other persons, even in some of the "wheels" of campus life (however, innate charm is a wonderful gift). Then there is the deeper level of natural interest in other students as human beings, who have the problems, the perplexities, the gifts, the handicaps and the possibilities that make them different, and fascinating to know. As you get a little older, you realize that even teachers are human beings with their own problems and possibilities, and finally that your parents also, as one student put it, "have a right to be understood."

When you being working and playing with children, you soon find them to be human, however improbable this may seem at first. They are not monsters, not darlings, but persons at their own growth level, and it is very important that you find out about and identify those levels so you may know what to expect. (Even so, they'll surprise you; teaching is never monotonous.) Adjusting to other students, to teachers, to children is best done at the deeper level of human interest, human sympathy, and, in the religious sense, human love. Go back for a moment to Kant's Ethical Imperative.[5] Understand yourself, your own best purposes, and serve those purposes with all your human powers. This implies the same obligation to understand other persons, young or old, friend or enemy, and do what you can to facilitate *their* progress toward their best purposes. You and Chuck go out to the tennis courts and start knocking balls around. As you get into play, you put out your best efforts—why? Pride? Desire to win? The sportsman's wish to play your best always? These are all in the picture. What the Ethical Imperative adds is consideration of Chuck. Suppose he is not as good as you—do you ease up on your drives to the back-hand corner, or other vulnerable areas? Not unless he is an absolute beginner: in that case you keep the ball in play, encourage him, take only most of the points. If he is almost as good as you are, you play your best because that not only serves your best purpose but also improves his game. If he is better than you, both of you play your best. Whatever your respective levels, you appreciate his good plays and tell him so. This is different from flattery which uses his weakness for your own purposes. This is recognizing that each of you has the same right to enjoy a good game. You avoid sarcasm (making him so mad he'll hit the balls out) because this spoils his enjoyment and the game is not as good as it could be.

In your relations with others—children, college men and women, teachers, parents, ask yourself: "Am I using them, or am I respecting them as persons?" Ask yourself: "Am I using my personality to get by, or am I developing my human powers to serve my best purposes?" It seems to the author that this hard test will serve you well in adjusting to others so that you may work and play with them effectively and happily.

---

[5] See p. 101.

## QUESTIONS

1. List your own *real* objectives in each of the courses you are now taking. Discuss with classmates.

2. When is concentration easiest for you: in listening to a class lecture, in listening to a discussion about a class lecture, in reading an assignment, or in writing a theme? Can you analyze why this is true in your case?

3. Illustrate the application of some principle you have learned in one of your social science classes. Do the same for a principle from one of your activity classes.

4. Which is a better measure of achievement, essay type or objective test? Why?

5. What part of the library is most familiar to you? Least familiar? Can you study there as well as in your own room? Why?

6. Bring to class cards with notes on any of this week's reference readings (from any course). Exchange with a classmate and check her cards for correct documentation.

7. List the books now in your own professional library. Give some sample titles from your own personal library.

8. Make out a detailed schedule for next week including study periods for each course you are taking. Try to live by it for the week, and report progress in your class discussion group.

9. How much sleep do you estimate was average for you (per night) last year? This year? How much do you think you need?

10. What age level do you get along with most successfully? Have you suggestions for improving your own skill in human relations?

11. Try a dramatization in class illustrating the ethical imperative in daily living (either positively or negatively). Each group decides on its own situation; dialogues and action are spontaneous, roles are played with consistency.

## SELECTED REFERENCES

Chandler, John R., G. C. Beamer, C. C. Williams, and V. L. Armstrong. *Successful Adjustment in College* (Englewood Cliffs: Prentice-Hall, 1951), Chaps. II and III.

Doane, C. J., P. J. VanderLinden, B. E. David, M. A. Bunson, and P. K. Vonk. *Introduction to College* (Boston: Allyn & Bacon, 1958), Pts. II and III.

Rice, Thurman B., and Fred V. Hein. *Living,* rev. ed. (Chicago: Scott Foresman, 1954), Chap. VII.

Turner, C. E. *Personal and Community Health,* 11th ed. (St. Louis: Mosby, 1959), Chaps. XIII, XV, XVI.

Van Dalen, Deobold, and Marcella Van Dalen. *The Health, Physical Education and Recreation Teacher* (Englewood Cliffs: Prentice-Hall, 1956), Chap. II.

Wessel, Janet. *Movement Fundamentals* (Englewood Cliffs: Prentice-Hall, 1957), Chaps. I, II, III.

Wilcox, Glenn W. *Basic Study Skills* (Boston: Allyn & Bacon, 1958), Chaps. II, V, VI.

# CHAPTER 6

# *The Growth of Our Profession*

THE TWO FRESHMEN were walking toward the gymnasium, talking with some heat about attitudes toward physical education. The leader of their quiz section in English had just elaborated his opinion that teaching English was a great field because ease of communication would promote intercultural understanding, and semantic difficulties were often an obstacle to good human relations. In the discussion that followed he had made light of most other major subjects, and physical education had come in for its share of criticism: it was nonacademic, an easy way to a degree, and outdated in a push-button world. The girls found their way into their adviser's office; there they poured out their troubles with a request to be transferred to another section, where their chosen profession might be viewed more sympathetically. More talk, however, brought out the fact that there were other possibilities.

1. It might be more intelligent to meet opposition than to run away from it.
2. It would help to understand personal reasons why some academically minded individuals might have a distaste for physical education, such as their own childhood incompetence

in games and resulting ridicule, with compensation through high grades in the rest of their school work. This might help the student appreciate an emotional reaction by others while substituting information for emotion in her own response.

3. Why not find out something about the place of physical education in other cultures so as to be able to write interesting themes about it—not the "History of Baseball" but discussions of such suggestions as these:

a. When early Roman schools began to borrow Greek educational ideas, why did they leave out music and physical education and concentrate on the "three R's"? Did this affect later educational theory?

b. How did the ideas of Plato and Aristotle and other Greek philosophers, about the oneness of mind and body and the balanced beauty of the harmonious person, compare with modern holistic [1] theories in the biological and social sciences?

c. Why did early church schools fail to include physical education? Was it the Roman tradition or the influence of asceticism?

d. What has been the effect of the Puritan tradition on the place of physical education in American schools?

4. It might be wise to get background information in physiology—the stress theory—and in the organismic school of psychology, that help to understand and express the contributions of physical education to mental as well as physical health, and to the development of personality.

5. It would be a good idea to find out more about the growth of physical education and the changing status of women in the United States, as well as the contribution of dis-

---

[1] Defined as the philosophic doctrine that *wholes* are determining factors, and not their constituent *parts*.

tinguished women who have been pioneers in various phases of physical education.

The rest of this chapter and the next, are developments of the last topic. They contain some familiar material, and much that would be difficult to find in any published history. The time division between the two chapters roughly coincides with the First World War. The chapters are structured to give brief background material in the general historical development of physical education in the United States, and changes in the status of women. There will be more detailed, but still brief, accounts of a few women pioneers at appropriate intervals. It would indeed be interesting, if space permitted, to describe the lives of all men and women pioneers in our field, for it is in the living struggles of individuals that history takes on reality. Since there is not time to study more of them, a selection of twelve women was made by the author, with the help of a number of her colleagues. Each of the twelve was instrumental in developing at least one important phase of our profession, although the work of each touched other phases as well as many lives. Each of the earlier workers also helped to break through the barriers society put in the way of women who were interested in careers. Thus each of them made a two-fold contribution: one to the development of a new field of education, the other to the expansion of women's sphere of living.

## Physical education in the United States before the Civil War

Colonial schools struggled to get enough school buildings and teachers to give the rudiments of the three R's and the catechism to American children, while early college courses trained in the classics for the ministry. Therefore physical education was an unfamiliar concept and remote from school curricula. Many men of prominence, however, mentioned its importance in their writing; Benjamin Franklin, Thomas Jefferson, and Noah Webster were among them. Children had little time, although plenty of inclination for games outside school, since their school day lasted from 8:00 to 12:00 in the morning and 2:00 to 6:00 in the afternoon. In the short time remaining for play, the academic intruded—at least in one school. The following regulation was in force in the William and Mary Grammar school: [2]

> If there are any sort of Plays or Diversions in Use among them which are not to be found extant in any Printed Books, let the Master compose and dictate to his Scholars Colloquies fit for all sorts of plays, that they may learn at all times to speak Latin in apt and proper terms.

Nor were games or amusements for children or adults looked on with favor in the early New England colonies except practice with bow and arrow and small arms, which had such practical outcomes as hunting for game and fishing. Later, as colonial life became more settled, and the English governors set up a social pattern like that of the parent country, many forms of recreation became acceptable. The Dutch in New Amsterdam, and the large landholders in the South, were much more tolerant of all kinds of amusement. They felt no religious strictures against swimming, skating, bowling on the green, riding, horse racing, and even dancing and card games. But, of course, none of these forms of recreation found their way into the instructional program of schools or colleges.

Much later, in the 1820's, a group of young intellectuals from Germany brought to this country enthusiasm for the gymnastics of Friedrich Ludwig Jahn—as well as a keen desire to escape political persecution. Jahn was a German leader of youth groups dedicated to political freedom and physical

---

[2] E. E. Brown, *The Making of Our Middle Schools* (New York: Longmans Green, 1910), p. 139. By permission.

strength for the sake of building a strong nation. Strength was pursued by vigorous gymnastics and apparatus work, at first spontaneously developed, and highly recreational in nature, later organized into the "German System" by Jahn's followers. Charles Follen at Harvard, Charles Beck at the Round Hill School in Northampton, and Francis Lieber at a public Gymnasium and swimming school in Boston, all introduced Jahn's gymnastics to apparently eager groups of participants. However the interest died down after a very few years, and was revived only by the large number of Germans entering this country in the 1840's and 1850's. These newcomers founded Turnvereine (gymnastic centers) in some of the larger cities of the midwest, and from their interest, German gymnastics appeared in the public schools of Kansas City, Cincinnati, St. Louis, Milwaukee, Chicago, Indianapolis, and other cities in the 1860's.

German gymnastics were considered altogether too strenuous for girls and women, and lighter forms of exercises were proposed by Catherine Beecher, whose career will be described later in the chapter. Another system was advocated by a popular lecturer on health, Dio Lewis, as "New gymnastics for old men, fat men, feeble men, young boys, and females of all ages." These lighter exercises were used in various groups, including some academies.

### Status of Women in the United States prior to the Civil War

Academies for girls were very rare institutions in the early days of our country. Either they were not strong enough, or not important enough as *persons* to be educated beyond the elementary grades. In the 1790's, so the story goes, an enraged voter in Haverhill, Massachusetts, confronted with a proposal to levy a tax for girls' education, said "Haverhill educate *She's?*

Never." [3] Boston itself did not open grammar schools to girls until 1789. Gradually more high schools in the East admitted girls, private "female seminaries" were founded, struggled with inadequate funds, and a few survived (among them were the Female Academy of Salem, North Carolina in 1802, The Troy Female Seminary in Troy, New York, in 1821, and the Mt. Holyoke Seminary in 1837). The next stage, college education for women, was initiated by Oberlin on a co-educational basis in 1833, followed by Antioch in 1853 and the State University of Iowa in 1855. In the East and South separate colleges for women were established: Georgia Female College, Mary Sharp College in Tennessee, Elmira College in New York —all before the Civil War.

Other phases of women's living were correspondingly limited as seen from our point of view, but doubtless not from theirs—they were too busily occupied within the limits. In the settled areas of the colonies and early eastern states, women's life was a domestic economy in which was done all the work of producing, clothing, feeding, and caring for a large family. Practically no services were provided from outside. The baby was born at home—no hospitals; his clothes had been made at home, often out of material woven at home; his food and that of all the family was prepared at home—no mixes—on a cook stove stoked by wood chopped at home—no coal, gas, or electricity. To help with these and other laborious processes of living were grandparents, maiden aunts, older daughters, or at higher income levels, domestic servants. There was also much church work to be done, and hospitality to be shown to visitors. Social life was complex, or less so, depending on the status of the family. A pattern of rigorous gentility was prescribed for the girl's early training in manners and morals. Details of the pattern could be found in print in many forms: Moody's *School of Good Manners,* Benjamin Franklin's *Poor Richard's Al-*

---

[3] Quoted in Inez Haynes Irwin, *Angels and Amazons: A Hundred Years of American Women* (New York: Doubleday Doran, 1933), p. 23.

*manac, The Lady's Pocket Diary,* and many others. Later, when Andrew Jackson's election to the Presidency and expanding opportunities to make money relaxed the rather closely drawn class lines of early American society, etiquette books became a "must" for those who wished to rise in station. These books discussed with great frankness problems of daily behavior: dress, eating, subjects of conversation, drawing-room manners, treatment of "menials," and the like. Relations with the other sex were of prime interest; even if engaged, a young lady was thus advised: [4]

> Accept not unnecessary assistance in putting on cloaks, shawls, over-shoes, or anything of the sort. . . . Read not out of the same book; let not your eagerness to see anything induce you to place your head close to another person's. . . . The waltz is a dance of too loose a character, and unmarried ladies should refrain from it altogether.

Out of doors also, her behavior must be circumspect: [5]

> In crossing the street a lady should gracefully raise her dress to the ankle, with one hand. To raise the dress with both hands is vulgar, except in places where the mud is very deep.
>
> Ladies are not allowed, upon ordinary occasions, to take the arm of any one but a relative or an accepted lover, in the street and in the daytime. However, in the evening, in the fields, or in a crowd, whenever she may need protection, she should not refuse it. She should merely pass her hand over the gentleman's arm.

At lower economic levels, young women were beginning to find a degree of economic independence. The textile mills of the eastern seaboard began to draw on women and children for their labor supply. They worked from sun up to sun down, as

---

[4] Quoted in Arthur Schlesinger, *Learning How to Behave* (New York: Macmillan, 1946), p. 25. By permission.

[5] Quoted in Kate Hevner Mueller, *Educating Women for a Changing World* (Minneapolis: University of Minnesota Press, 1954), pp. 43–44. By permission.

the men did, but for much smaller wages. Even so, by 1831, 39,000 women were earning more than $4,000,000 annually in the cotton factories, and their wages appeared to be "so much clear gain to the country as well as substantial benefit to their parents." [6]

Woman's life on the westward moving frontier, and in the sparsely settled areas following the frontier, was a different existence entirely. No room here, nor time to train the "cherished flowers" of eastern seaboard society. Women did what had to be done, sharing burdens equally with their men as far as their strength permitted. Added to the household tasks already described were outdoor jobs. The cabin clearing had to be cultivated; while the men were taking out more trees, the women did primitive agriculture with hand tools. Stock, if any, had to be tended, and the home food supply processed from the seed or the hoof to the table. On occasions when the man was working at some distance from the cabin, or gone to the nearest settlement for supplies, the woman must be ready for home-guard duty, against emergencies and against Indians in some areas. Her increasing brood of children (the annual increment brought most frontier families to ten or more) got whatever education they had from their mother. The self-reliant women of the West may have been reared in a set pattern of gentility, but necessity imposed on them a more practical though equally moral way of living. They had to accept responsibility for all phases of survival, equal to the burden borne by their husbands. It is, therefore, understandable that many of the first steps toward women's freedom, such as co-education, were taken in the West.

The health of the "cherished flowers" of Eastern gentility was considered very delicate. Nor did the frontierswoman have the health and vigor to enable her to live out a long life of hard-

---

[6] Mary Beard, *America through Women's Eyes* (New York: Macmillan, 1933), p. 131.

ship. Catherine Beecher declared that American women were
in a bad way: [7]

> Every year I hear more and more complaints of the poor health
> that is so very common among grown people, especially among
> women. And physicians say, that this is an evil that is constantly
> increasing, so that they fear ere long, there will be no healthy
> women in the country.

Miss Beecher's concern for the health of women, and of
children as well, led to an interest in calisthenics to secure the
"health, strength, and beauty of the physical system." [8] She
was the first of a number of dedicated women who saw and
worked for this need. She is the first pioneer whose life we shall
consider in some detail.

### Catherine Beecher (1800–78) Pioneer evangelist in the education and physical education of children, girls, and women.

When the well-known New England clergyman, Lyman
Beecher, was married for the second time, the oldest of his ten
children was eighteen. This was Catherine, a "fine-looking girl,
abundantly endowed with intellect, exuberant spirits, and
abounding vitality." [9] All of her resources were needed when
she had to meet the second tragedy of her life, the death of her
fiance who was drowned while crossing the Atlantic. By her
own strength and the sympathetic help of her family, she came
through this experience without loss of her intense religious
faith, but with great need for work that would be completely
absorbing. So she threw herself with fervor into teaching,

---

[7] Catherine Beecher, *Letters to the People on Health and Happiness,* 1856.
Quoted in Willystine Goodsell, *Pioneers of Women's Education in the United
States* (New York: McGraw-Hill, 1931), p. 200. By permission.

[8] Catherine Beecher, *Physiology and Calisthenics for Schools and Families*
(New York: Harper, 1856), p. IV.

[9] Lyman Beecher Stowe, *Saints, Sinners, and Beechers* (Indianapolis:
Bobbs-Merrill, 1934), p. 110. By permission.

building up education for girls and young women, writing and lecturing as a kind of "educational evangelist." Others of that famous family were to become evangelists also: Harriet Beecher Stowe was to rock the country with *Uncle Tom's Cabin,* and Henry Ward Beecher spoke out for emancipation in no uncertain terms from his pulpit in Plymouth Congregational Church of Brooklyn.

Catherine Beecher's writings were widely published. *Domestic Economy* and *Physiology and Calisthenics* became best sellers, and during her busy life she had more than a dozen other books published, as well as countless articles. Her first school, a "Female Seminary" in Hartford, Connecticut, opened in 1823. There were tried many innovations: domestic economy, student government, and a program of calisthenics, to promote the "well-balanced mind in a healthy body." Miss Beecher described the latter:

> The attempt to remedy physical defects came about in this manner. An English lady of fine person and manner came to us as a teacher of what then had no name, but now would be called calisthenics. She gave a large number of the exercises that are in my work on *Physiology and Calisthenics.* From this came the system of Calisthenics which I invented, which spread all over the country.[10]

During the next three decades Miss Beecher carried education for women, like a banner, to the Middle West: to Ohio, Iowa, and Wisconsin. (In Milwaukee she founded a school later to become Milwaukee-Downer College.) In 1852, she organized the American Women's Educational Association, in order to promote higher education for women, including teacher training institutions. (This year of 1852 was a busy one for the Beechers. Catherine's father published *Views on Theology;* brother Edward, *Conflict of the Ages;* sister Harriet, *Uncle*

---

[10] Stowe, *op.cit.,* p. 78. By permission.

*Tom's Cabin;* and brother Henry Ward was writing his "Star Papers" for *The Independent,* which gave him national leadership in the cause of the Union.) For more than twenty years the American Women's Educational Association flourished, broadening its scope in 1873 to "secure the proper training of the daughters of the industrial classes for their future duties as housekeepers, wives, mothers, nurses of infants and the sick, and also all domestic helpers needed in these various departments, and, as far as practicable, to do this in connection with our schools." [11]

Although she had put her own health under terrific strain with overwork, nothing could weaken the resistless force of Catherine Beecher's personality. An amusing story was told by President White of Cornell University about her persistence even when in her 1870's. She had, it seemed, found a course in the Cornell catalogue that she wanted to take—and she appeared in the president's office to inform him of the fact. Somewhat embarrassed, he said that the University had no courses open to women.[12]

> "Oh, that is quite all right, Dr. White, in fact I prefer to take it with men," she disarmingly replied. That question seeming to be settled, Dr. White inquired whether he could be of service in finding her a place to lodge in town?
>
> "No, thank you, Dr. White," she answered, "I shall room in ——," mentioning one of the dormitories on the campus. "But, Miss Beecher," protested Dr. White, "that is a dormitory for young men, it has no accommodations for ladies!" "I have inspected the accommodations, and find them entirely satisfactory," imperturbably replied Miss Beecher. "And as for those young men, who are of appropriate ages to be my grandsons, they will not trouble me in the least." She stayed, took the course, roomed in the dormitory, and became one of the most popular inmates of the building.

---

[11] Stowe, *op.cit.,* p. 130.
[12] *Ibid.,* p. 129. By permission.

What were Catherine Beecher's calisthenics like? In one of her books she describes them: [13]

> This system is arranged on *scientific principles* with the design of exercising *all* the muscles, and exercising them *equally* and *harmoniously*. It embraces most of what is to be found in the French and English works that exhibit the system of *Ling,* the celebrated Swedish Professor, whose method has been widely adopted in European schools and Universities.
>
> It also contains, in addition, many valuable exercises that have been employed in Health Establishments for the cure of disease and deformities.

How much influence did this system of calisthenics have on the future of physical education? It is hard to estimate from this distance in time, but it is certain that her books had a wide distribution; none were more popular than her writings on the alarming state of health in the United States, and the cure in the form of exercises based on the knowledge of physiology. In the opinion of Willystine Goodsell, these writings "played their part in opening the minds of the American people to the need of physical training and health education in the schools." [14]

## Physical education in the United States from 1860–1914

The Civil War, like all wars, stimulated the rate of change in American society and its economic base. The postwar period differed markedly in the North and in the South. The South was physically devastated, and in a condition of political and economic chaos that yielded only gradually to reconstruction through a long and painful period. The North expanded explosively: in population, in the increase of industrialization in

---

[13] Catherine Beecher, *Letters to the People on Health and Happiness.* Quoted in Goodsell, *op.cit.,* p. 210.
[14] Goodsell, *op.cit.,* p. 215.

the East and Middle West, in settlement of the great plains and the West Coast, in production of agricultural and mineral products, and in the network of trade and transportation binding the country together. Money was there for the making, great fortunes were established, but panics and business failures were also in the picture.

Education expanded also: secondary education increased, school housing improved, and the curriculum broadened in scope. Physical education benefited by these changes. Already introduced, as we have seen, into some schools and colleges, it became an accepted part of the college curriculum through the work of such leaders as Edward Hitchcock who started the program at Amherst in 1861, and Dudley Allen Sargent who went to direct the new gymnasium at Harvard in 1879. Dio Lewis, a popular but by no means scientific lecturer on health reforms, had started a short-lived teacher training school for physical education in Boston in 1861, and the Turner society began to train gymnastic leaders in Rochester in the same year. Their school closed for the duration of the war, then re-opened in New York. However, it furnished leaders for the Turnverine in the cities with German populations, and only later sent teachers to the public schools. In 1881 Sargent began his long and productive career of teacher training in his private school in Cambridge; in 1885 Robert J. Roberts started a two year course at Springfield College for Y.M.C.A. gymnastic leaders; in 1886 Dr. Wlliam Anderson and Dr. Watson Savage began their respective professional schools. Harvard and Chatauqua offered their first summer courses about this time, and the Boston Normal School of Gymnastics, under the direction of Amy Morris Homans, was founded in 1888, as described later in this chapter. For many years most teacher training institutions in physical education were privately supported schools offering two- or three-year courses. Gradually colleges, state normal schools, and universities instituted short diploma courses, then four-year curricula leading to the B.A. with specialization in

## Probably invented by Dio Lewis

physical education. Among the early ones were the Universities of Washington, Nebraska, California, Missouri, and Oberlin College.

Meanwhile a new system of gymnastics was brought to the United States from Sweden by Hartvig Nissen, in 1873, and Baron Nils Posse a few years later. Like German gymnastics, the Swedish system was developed in its own country by an intensely patriotic leader in response to the threat of Napoleonic conquest. The gymnastic system of each leader—Friedrich, Ludwig Jahn and Per Henrik Ling—was an effort to improve the health and strength of his country's youth, and so the national manpower. There, however, the resemblance ceased. Ling based the Swedish system on his studies of anatomy and physiology; rudimentary as these sciences were in the early 1800's, there was justification *at that time* for the claim that Swedish Gymnastics was founded on scientific principles. Jahn, the German leader, was concerned with getting young men interested in developing their own health and strength, and much of the German apparatus work had a stuntlike quality that did hold interest. To us, some 150 years later, both systems seem similarly formal and artificial as mass drills, and difficult as apparatus exercises. But to the proponents of each system in the 1800's, the differences were as day and night, and a "battle of the systems" resulted that raged in the contemporary literature and meetings, both in Europe and in this country.

Physical education developed slowly in the public schools, although it had made an early start in many private academies. California passed a law in 1866 linking physical exercises with the laws of health as desirable parts of the school program. In the 1880's a number of cities introduced physical education in their schools, and in 1892 Ohio required it by law. This was followed by somewhat similar legislation in Wisconsin (1897), North Dakota (1899), Pennsylvania (1901), Michigan (1911), and Idaho (1913).[15] The early school and college programs were largely gymnastics, occasionally livened by games. In the men's colleges athletics developed rapidly under student management, and entirely apart from physical education. Just as rapidly grew various problems of intercollegiate athletic competition: schedules, rules, officiating, amateurism, and injuries. In 1905 football was nearly banished from the college scene because of injuries and irregularities. It was saved after a joint meeting of representatives from 28 colleges resulted in faculty control under an association later known as the NCAA (National Collegiate Athletic Association), which has had not only long life but great influence over the conduct of college athletics. High schools followed the college example, bringing some semblance of order out of easy going practices that permitted anyone, principal, janitor, or transient athlete, to compete on the school team. Associations were formed in

---

[15] Deobold Van Dalen, Elmer Mitchell, and Bruce Bennett, *A World History of Physical Education* (Englewood Cliffs, N.J.: Prentice-Hall, 1953), p. 397.

many states, beginning with Wisconsin, Michigan, Illinois, and Indiana, to regulate interscholastic competition.

The physical education program for girls and women, on the other hand, included athletic sports as they developed, and kept them controlled for educational outcomes, as we shall see later.

College and school health programs began with medical examinations in the colleges, and health inspection in the schools, largely as preventive measures. The men's colleges checked on the condition of their athletes, and used Sargent's anthropometric tests as a basis for encouraging symmetrical body development. The women's colleges were concerned lest the "delicate health" of their students be impaired by college work, and provided medical supervision and care as well as examinations. Epidemics of small pox in San Antonio and diphtheria in Boston forced larger cities to appoint school physicians who began to inspect for contagious disease, as often as

### Swedish corrective gymnastics

*State University of Iowa*

feasible. Soon the inspections became more complete examinations; by 1915 these examinations were required by state legislation in 26 states. Health instruction in the early days was linked to the temperance movement, and legislation compelling instruction in the effects of alcohol and narcotics spread widely. Another agency promoting health instruction at this time was the tuberculosis association. In the first decade of the twentieth century new school buildings were much more hygienically constructed, with better ventilation, lighting, adjustable seats, and sanitary drinking fountains.

Recreation as an organized institution had its beginnings in small public squares and city parks early in the history of most urban centers. These were not used for play, however; in fact play was generally forbidden, as illustrated in a Chicago city ordinance of 1851: [16]

> No person shall play at ball, cricket, or at any other game or play whatsoever in any of the enclosed public parks or grounds in this city, under penalty of $5.00 for every offense.

The playground movement came later, when American cities began to recognize the problems of poverty areas and the importance of play for all children. Playgrounds for children of the slums were seen as a civic necessity, and provided by many private welfare agencies toward the close of the nineteenth century.[17] Sand gardens for small children were established in Boston in 1885, followed later by the Charlesbank playground for older children and youth in the same city. As the movement spread, city governments supported playgrounds, and early in the twentieth century a small park development in the South Park District of Chicago gave a revolutionary impetus to the expansion of public recreation. These landscaped, well-

---

[16] Elizabeth Halsey, *Development of Public Recreation in Metropolitan Chicago* (Chicago: Chicago Recreation Commission, 1940), p. 8.
[17] *Ibid.*, p. 30.

equipped, well-staffed ten-acre areas provided programs for all ages at all seasons. When the newly organized Playground and Recreation Association of America held its first annual convention in Chicago in 1907 President Theodore Roosevelt sent out a call to the meeting, urging mayors of all municipalities to send their representatives so they might see these parks, which he described as "one of the most notable civic achievements of any American City." [18]

## Status of women in the United States 1860–1914

Just as the Civil War initiated changes in education and physical education, so it affected the status of women. Great demands were made on their time, strength, and ability. They organized relief work, collected money, bandages, and clothing to be sent to local depots of the United States Sanitary Commission, which was the early counterpart of the Red Cross. They did evangelical work among the soldiers under the Christian Commission, established Soldiers' Rests at railway junctions to care for the needs of soldiers in transit, and served as volunteer nurses at base hospitals and even at the front. Speaking of their war work President Lincoln said: [19]

I have never studied the art of paying compliments to women; but I must say that if all that has been said by orators and poets since the creation of the world were applied to the women of America, it would not do them justice for their conduct during this war.

Also in their own home situations, while men were at the front, women kept the business, the farm, the plantation going. At the same time manufacturers of war materials drew single women in increasing numbers into their labor

[18] *Halsey, op.cit.,* p. 31.
[19] As quoted in Arthur Meier Schlesinger, *New Viewpoints in American History* (New York: Macmillan, 1948), p. 144. By permission.

supply. After the war many women in industry stayed there, while married women returned to the distaff side of home production. There remained a comparatively large number in domestic service and farm work. However, in 1870, only one woman in ten was gainfully employed, and only one worker in seven was a woman.[20] These figures contrast sharply with those of today, when one (plus) woman in three is gainfully employed, and one worker in three is a woman. What did these employed women of the 1870's do? The top five occupations, in number of women engaged in them, were domestic servants, agricultural laborers, dressmakers and milliners, teachers, and mill operatives. Most young women who were attracted to professions went into teaching—90 per cent of them. In the entire country there was but one woman architect, 25 dentists, 43 librarians, 13 designers, and 43 reporters.[21]

The work of women in the home remained laborious and time-consuming in comparison with modern procedures. Indoor plumbing was used in better urban residences; food care and preparation were eased somewhat by the general use of ice boxes, and, later on, gas stoves for cooking. One time-consuming job—the cleaning and filling of kerosene lamps—was eliminated for city homes as electricity became available for lighting in the early decades of the twentieth century. Materials for clothing no longer were woven in the home, although many of the clothes were made in the seasonal sewing bouts with the itinerant dressmaker and gossip column who stayed for days at a time. Large families lived in houses as large as they could maintain, and had the help of as many servants as they could afford. Even small houses often sheltered spinster aunts and grandparents who gave some help to domestic enterprises, and were baby sitters as a matter of course.

---

[20] *Occupations of Women through Seven Decades* (Washington: U.S. Department of Labor, Women's Bureau, 1947), p. 34.
[21] *Ibid.*, p. 156.

It was, therefore, a little easier for women to get away from the home into an area of developing social freedom. Space does not let us describe all the milestones marking the way toward this freedom, but some of them should be noted.

1. The dynamism of the women who found themselves working together in patriotic or humane causes during the Civil War stimulated them to continue in reform movements after the war.

2. Women's clubs were organized for a variety of purposes, in addition to societies for church work which had existed for centuries. The Farmers' Grange movement, organized in the mid-west in 1867, was co-educational from its beginning—a provision contributing greatly to its strength.[22]

3. Feminism, organized to promote the rights of women, was chiefly involved with the battle for women's suffrage. Initiating the struggle was the Seneca Falls meeting of 1848, when a call to a women's rights convention secured a large response and a very vigorous meeting. In spite of ridicule from press and even from the pulpit, annual meetings were held until the war, and the movement gained strength. Not enough strength was gained, however, to permit women to secure the franchise along with Negro males when the Fifteenth Amendment was passed. They then began to win state suffrage laws, beginning with the state of Wyoming, which organized as a territory in 1869, giving equal political rights to men and women, and was admitted to the Union in 1890. Finally, as other states followed suit, and as women's influence grew, the equal suffrage amendment to the United States constitution was passed in 1920.

4. Legal rights: to own and manage their own property, to have custody of their children, to make contracts and bring suit,

[22] Ernest Groves, *The American Woman* (New York: Greenberg, 1937), p. 260.

were gradually acquired. In colonial and early federal courts a woman had about the same rights as a minor, but by the turn of the twentieth century, the principle of equal rights was generally recognized if not always give actual legal form.

5.  Dress reform, or efforts toward it, accompanied the other "emancipation movements." The hoop skirts and twenty-two-inch waists of the 1860's not only limited women's movements, but were also unkind to their health and comfort. Mrs. Amelia Bloomer set the example of abandoning skirts in favor of the garment that took her name. This was a form of Turkish trousers, cut so voluminously that when the wearer stood still they appeared to be a skirt coming to the shoe tops. But as she moved it became obvious that this woman must have two legs as well as two feet. Such a daring revelation was altogether too much for public opinion, and bloomers were out—to be revived when needed at a later period by bicycle riders and young women exercising in the gymnasium. Somehow women lived through the era of the bustle, and the contorted posture of the "Grecian bend." By the turn of the century, the "Gibson girl" became the prototype of the "New Woman." She played golf in heavy woolen skirts that actually cleared the ground, crisp high-necked shirtwaists, and low-heeled shoes. But women rode astride only on the farm or in the far west, and they tried to play field hockey in skirts so long that the ball was in hiding, as well as the players' "limbs."

6.  Educational opportunities were opening up fairly generally before 1914, although in 1870 college education for women was vigorously and sincerely opposed by many men (and women) as being destructive of women's health and feminine qualities. In the 70's President Eliot of Harvard quoted the opinion of leading scientific and medical authorities that women could not bear the stress put upon men in college.[23]

---

[23] *Groves, op.cit.,* p. 318.

The Reverend John Todd, in an article written in 1871, posed this question.[24]

> Is it certain that the delicate, nervous, physical organization of women is such (I admit all you ask as to her quickness of mind and fine mental attributes) that she can endure the physical strain requisite for a regular, old-fashioned college course? I am informed that in institutions where the experiment has been tried, of 100 young men who are fitted for college, 66 go through the course. Out of 100 females *only 6* go through the course. Exceptions there may be, but as a general thing, can the female constitution bear the long strain?

In spite of objections and obstacles, girls and women have gone to high school and college in increasing numbers, following the general national trend toward more years of formal education. Physical education for women, however, was still limited. By no wild stretch of the imagination may we picture a modern freshman, in shorts, running around a college gymnasium in the 1870's. No, the college woman of that day was lucky if she had a college gymnasium, or any space for games. She was fortunate if anyone in the college thought it important that she should have physical education. Such programs, and such facilities were by no means general. Household duties were accepted as sufficient exercise in some schools, and training in graceful movement and deportment in others. Many of the young colleges adopted curricula identical to those of the men's colleges except for gymnastics and athletics, which would have put too much strain on the "delicate female constitution." We have described the efforts of Catherine Beecher to devise suitable calisthenics, and to introduce physical education as a part of education for children, girls, and women. The dedicated work and sincere convictions of other women expanded and improved this program in the years following Miss Beecher's life.

---

[24] *Ibid.*, p. 315. By permission.

*Amy Morris Homans (1848–1933) Pioneer in the professional education of teachers*

A young New England woman, teaching in a North Carolina school, heard two small boys plotting outside the open window:

"I'd like to scare Miss Homans."

"How'd you do that?"

"I'd bring my kitty to school and hide it in her desk. When she looked in maybe she'd jump."

"She would not—she'd just say [imitating the teacher's calm Northern accent] 'My! My! Whose little kitty is this?' "

This was one of Miss Homans' favorite stories, told to her young professional students to illustrate what she meant when she said: "Always be collected, and you will never be at a disadvantage."

In her early teaching experience Amy Morris Homans met the distinguished Boston philanthropist Mrs. Mary Hemenway. A great deal of wealth was at the latter's service; through her generosity and wise business management it served thousands of others in a number of educational and civic projects. To help her in the planning and administration of these enterprises, Mrs. Hemenway in 1877 secured the services of the "collected" young teacher as an executive assistant. Together they saved Old South Church in Boston (which was about to be razed for commercial purposes), established Old South Patriotic Prize Essays, and Old South Lecture series. They had cooking and sewing lessons started in the Boston public schools, and followed this up by establishing the Boston Normal School of Household Arts, later taken over as part of the Framingham State Normal School. Other forms of aid to individual schools and to societies of teachers followed. A few years later a young Swedish nobleman, Baron Nils Posse, presented a letter of introduction from a mutual acquaintance to Mrs. Hemenway. Baron Posse was a graduate of the military branch of the Royal

Central Gymnastic Institute of Stockholm, and an extremely personable young officer. He convinced the two collaborators that Swedish gymnastics would be a valuable part of any school program; consequently they decided to have this new work for children introduced to teachers in the Boston schools. So they engaged Baron Posse to give a series of lessons to those teachers and principals who wished to take them: some 140 did so, with great interest.[25] In 1888 and 1889 a two-year course for a selected group of teachers followed, and this grew into the Boston Normal School of Gymnastics.[26] Meanwhile plans were developed for an event of great importance to our profession: the first large meeting on physical education held in this country. With financial backing from Mrs. Hemenway, and executive direction by Miss Homans, it was carried out on an impressive scale. A distinguished committee of 61 men and women issued the "call" to a "conference in the interest of physical training" to be held in Boston November 29 and 30, 1889. The presiding officer was the United States Commissioner of Education, Dr. W. T. Harris. Different systems of physical education were demonstrated, papers on medical aspects of the work were given, and leaders of the International Sports Movement came from France and England to address the meeting, which drew some 2,000 interested participants. According to Dr. Skarstrom the conference had far-reaching effects, not the least of which was to change the general concept from physical training to physical education.[27]

Following the conference, in 1890 Miss Homans and Mrs. Hemenway persuaded the Boston school officials to put Swedish gymnastics into the elementary and secondary schools, under the able directorship of Dr. Edward Hartwell. At Mrs. Hemenway's death in 1894 the Boston Normal School of Gymnas-

[25] William Skarstrom, "Life and Work of Amy Morris Homans," in *Supplement to Research Quarterly,* AAHPER, **12** (October 1941), p. 615.

[26] Referred to in later pages as BNSG.

[27] Skarstrom, *op.cit.,* p. 619.

tics was underwritten for fifteen years by a provision of her
will, Miss Homans to continue as its head. At the end of this
period, which was marked by steady growth, the school became
the Department of Hygiene and Physical Education at Wellesley College. It was housed in the present Mary Hemenway
Hall, which was built in 1909, by large and small gifts from
friends and graduates of the BNSG. In 1917 it became a graduate course, and in this form was a leader among professional
courses in our field for many years. However, in 1954 financial
limitations as well as restrictions of a narrowing academic
policy closed the professional work of the department. In 1918
Miss Homans retired, at the age of seventy, to a very busy
private life. She traveled, spoke to alumnae groups as well as
to students, helped to raise funds for scholarships and for the
proposed swimming pool and recreation building. During her
life two honorary degrees were conferred on her.[28] She was one
of the first group of recipients of the annual Honor Award of
the AAHPER and among the first dozen members to be
elected to the American Academy of Physical Education.

This was a productive life in terms of work done; a tre-
mendously respected career as measured by public recognition
and honors awarded. Beyond these tangible accomplishments
survives the growing influence of Miss Homans' teaching,
through the work of her graduates, and, in turn, of their
graduates. Many well-recognized departments of physical
education have had BNSG or Wellesley graduates as administrators and staff members. Alumnae of "the school" evaluate its
influence highly. From the first Miss Homans set a high standard of excellence in academic and professional teaching. When
the BNSG broadened its curriculum to include academic requirements, it drew on the services of such illustrious Harvard
faculty members as Josiah Royce in philosophy, Dr. H. P.

---

[28] An M.A. from Bates college and Doctor of Pedagogy from Russell Sage
College.

Bowditch, dean of the College of Medicine, in anthropometry, Dr. William Conant in anatomy, as well as various faculty members from the Massachusetts Institute of Technology: Dr. W. T. Sedgwick in hygiene and biology, and Dr. T. Hough in physiology.[29] Later, as a department of Wellesley College, it not only had the resources of that college faculty, but developed also a fine departmental faculty.

A close second to professional excellence in the school's teaching was a very high standard of conduct and social poise. A wondrous example of poise herself, erect, elegantly dressed in black, white hair meticulously groomed, Miss Homans gave the impression of a ship under full sail as she moved about the building. Two years was a short time to make a dignified teacher out of a high-spirited youngster fresh from preparatory or high school. This growing up process was hastened by group talks and personal interviews with Miss Homans herself. These famous occasions were the source of legends told to this day by alumnae. At the time they were always fear-inspiring, and often painful, because Miss Homans believed in what she called the "direct method." This legacy from early days of New England discipline usually took the form of a quiet but incisive and complete rehearsal of the student's failings, heard by the culprit in dazed silence. Often the youngster did not realize the import of the few well-chosen, encouraging words that closed the interview. Some students did not discover Miss Homans' warm and friendly interest until they achieved senior or alumna status. Nor did they all know her engaging sense of humor, so delightfully aided by her sister "Miss Gertrude," who could make light of any problem, even her own deafness.

Miss Homans' modern viewpoint as well as her basic idealism are well expressed in these words from her talk to the alumnae at their annual meeting June 15, 1929: [30]

[29] Catalogues of the Boston Normal School of Gymnastics 1891–1909.

[30] *Bulletin of the Mary Hemenway Alumnae Association,* September 1929, p. 3.

In the activities of physical education the young human reveals and expresses his fundamental self perhaps more truly and completely than in any other way. Through the wise guidance and leadership of such activities, and in the close and friendly relations they engender, the teacher has unsurpassed opportunities to present ideals of "the good life" as regards health and efficiency, thoroughness, perseverance, and high quality of action, unselfish, courteous and honorable conduct.

The feelings of alumnae and colleagues were set out in the minutes of the National Association for the Physical Education of College Women April 17, 1934, following her death October 29, 1933.

When the physical presence of a great leader is withdrawn, the essence of her spirit which is left to us becomes more real. Through the power of her spirit Amy Morris Homans built a structure of influence which will endure. It is a structure harmonious because she had serenity and poise, balanced because she had stability of judgment, well-proportioned because she had a vision of the growth of the profession through the growth of its members in all phases of living.

This association owes its existence to Miss Homans, for it was through her planning and effort that we first came together. At that time she was elected our honorary member. It is, therefore, fitting that we recognize, however inadequately, our debt to her. But it is more than mere recognition that we wish to express. We have lost a friend who was always warmly interested in our problems, sound in her advice, far-sighted in forecasting the results of our decisions, and humanly generous in the gift of her experience. Our own sorrow at this loss should be tempered by the example of her courage. The hard things which Miss Homans had to meet, which come the way of every idealist who achieves, were always faced squarely. There was no drawing back in her code. She went on through the years, showing us the meaning of "the last of life, for which the first was made."

Every one of us, directly or indirectly, has been enriched by the dignity given to our work by her life. It would be her wish to have each of us feel that Amy Morris Homans is still her friend.

## Delphine Hanna (1854–1941) Pioneer in College Physical Education

Oberlin College, its alumni are proud to say, has a fine record of enterprise and innovation. Not the least of these innovations, certainly from our point of view, was its action in 1885 when it invested $300 for the year's salary and expenses of a serious young teacher of physical education, Delphine Hanna.[31] Like other pioneers in the field Miss Hanna was impressed with the poor health of children she had been teaching. She believed that a scientific application of the new programs in gymnastics might help them. First approaching Dio Lewis, she found his theory and work popular rather than scientific. Next she enrolled in Dr. Sargent's teachers' course in Cambridge, and while there studied with prominent orthopedists in Boston. These qualifications brought her to the attention of the Oberlin officials who were looking for someone to take charge of the program in the new wing of Ladies' Hall, which had a women's gymnasium on the first floor.

The position at Oberlin was not an easy one. Among the obstacles were limited funds (increased by a gift for equipment) a small gymnasium, primitive living conditions for herself, and the usual uphill road of building up a new subject on a college campus. However, obstacles seemed only to stimulate this indefatigable young woman. Within the next eighteen years she had recorded and published anthropometric data on 1,600 college women, had completed medical school at the University of Michigan in two years, and had later (!) earned

---

[31] For most of the material on Delphine Hanna I am indebted to Dr. Minnie Lynn, whose M.A. thesis on the life of Dr. Hanna is an illuminating contribution to the history of physical education. Minnie Lynn, "Portrait of a Pioneer," *Oberlin Alumni Magazine* (July 1957), p. 22.

## Basketball in the Gay Nineties

a B.A. degree from Cornell University and received an honorary M.A. from Oberlin. On the job, she had expanded a diploma training course of one year to one of the first four-year curricula for physical education teachers leading to the B.A. degree, and had become the first woman to attain professorial rank in physical education when Oberlin promoted her to that status in 1903.

Among her professional students were many who have added to the growth of our program; an early group of men students included Thomas D. Wood, Fred A. Leonard, and Luther Halsey Gulick.[32] Later Jesse F. Williams and J. B. Nash graduated from Oberlin. Perhaps the best known of the women whom she taught is Dr. Gertrude Moulton, who administered the department for many years after Dr. Hanna's retirement. Countless others have carried Dr. Hanna's teachings all over the country, and have served the profession well. They were

[32] Lynn, *op.cit.*, p. 24.

well grounded in the field of prescriptive exercise and massage, and so able to serve efficiently as therapists in the First World War.

Her college program was in no way limited to the professional students. From the beginning she used anthropometric data to plan individual work as needed, for all college women. She also encouraged a broad program of sports, and organized an association that preceded our present WRA groups. In those days it was called the Gymnasium and Field Association, founded in 1904. She foresaw the camping movement, and was responsible for establishing a college camp on the shores of Lake Erie, financed by an endowment as well as by the sale of neighboring lots to Oberlin faculty members.

The alumnae have recently established the Delphine Hanna Foundation "for her profound influence and constructive leadership in physical education." [33] Dr. Hanna belonged to many organizations and was active in them. She was honored in many ways: selected for the Michigan Hall of Fame in 1925, and given the annual Honor Award of the AAHPER in 1931. "She was a pioneer in deed, thought, and vision for the future." [34]

## Clelia Duel Mosher (1863–1940) Pioneer in research and writing

We are prone to think that research and writing are very recent developments in our field, and certainly the growth of scientific work in the last twenty years has been phenomenal. Many women are making excellent contributions at the present time, and some of them are directing the work of graduate students in fruitful investigations. Years ago a pioneer in research set an example to workers in our day—an example of indefatigable study, careful check of findings before publishing, and ultimate sharing of results through the discipline of writing

[33] *Ibid.*, p. 24.
[34] *Supplement to Research Quarterly, op.cit.*, p. 652.

for publication. Intellectual interests came to Clelia Mosher naturally. A long line of ancestors leading back to early American times were leaders in medicine, ministry, teaching, and fine arts. Although she was a frail youngster, and her physician father feared that her health would not take her very far in school, she was so well equipped with drive and determination that she never stopped studying! She completed the B.A. at Stanford, where she had laboratory training in the biological sciences, and became an assistant in hygiene. Almost at once she began to study women's respiration. The data and conclusions of her M.A. thesis on this subject challenged the contemporary texts in physiology, which agreed that women breathed costally, men, diaphragmatically. Her conclusion in 1894, that "there is no sexual difference in the type of respiration" was corroborated by Fitz of Harvard in 1896. Dr. Mosher's study led her to an interest in the restrictive clothing worn by women, and its effect upon their menstrual health. While teaching full time at Stanford she kept serial records of menstrual histories on some 400 normal women. In 1901 she published tentative conclusions as to the causes of menstrual disability: constricting clothing, inactivity, constipation, and the general assumption that discomfort, if not pain was inevitable. It is difficult to realize now that menstruation was then regarded as a form of illness, called, actually, the "sick time." Most women wore a thirteen-foot wide woolen skirt plus an amazing number of undergarments and a heavy corset; all this weight was suspended from a tightly constricted "wasp" waist, and lugged around for some fifteen hours a day. No wonder a serious student of the effects of this fashionable but nonsensical panoply became interested in dress reform. Miss Mosher urged college students to wear clothes that would permit enjoyment, not only of sports but of any movement.

Eager to find out more about the human mechanism, Clelia Mosher studied medicine at Johns Hopkins. After graduation she practiced medicine at Palo Alto, then became medical adviser to women and director of the Roble gymnasium at Stanford.[35] Continuing her research and applying her conclusions to the practical problems of remedial work, she devised abdominal exercises that are used to this day, and still known by her name. Her book *Personal Hygiene for Women,* her other publications describing studies of the physical efficiency of women, and her method of recording posture known as the schematograph, have all been of great influence in our field.

Dr. Mosher's teaching (but not all of her writing) was interrupted by her extraordinarily valuable service in France in World War I, as Associate Medical Director of the Bureau of Refugees and Relief. On her return she continued a long-time project: comparative anthropometric studies of increases in height and weight among college women of Stanford, Vassar, and Smith over a period of some thirty years.

In addition to her scientific work, she had "extraordinary personal influence with girls": [36]

It is literally true that thousands of women bless her for their health and happiness. During her teaching years she was never too tired nor too impatient to listen to the ailments and difficulties of her students. She was always inventing ways to develop their courage—to give them belief in the sources of strength within themselves. She set up in their minds ideals of strength and beauty that had never before been taught.

### Senda Berenson Abbott (1868–1954) Pioneer in women's sports: Basketball

Study the picture of the charming ingenue of the "Gay Nineties" on page 157. This was Senda Berenson in her second year of study at the Boston Normal School of Gymnastics (1892)

---

[35] *Supplement to Research Quarterly, op.cit.,* p. 638.
[36] *Ibid.,* p. 643.

just before she began her memorable years of teaching at Smith College. Two years later she would be writing an enthusiastic article about the new game of basketball and its possibilities as a sport for women. When Smith College needed a teacher for the new program made possible by the recently completed gymnasium, Miss Homans recommended this young person. It proved a most strategic choice. Senda Berenson was an inspired teacher, according to the testimony of all who knew her. Part of the inspiration came from a deep conviction of the value of physical education. Her own work at BNSG was undertaken because of distressing physical weakness: she was unable to practice the piano, which she loved, because of an aching back. Progress is best told in her own words.[37]

How I hated that school for the first few months! Disliking all sciences, I studied anatomy, physiology, and so forth. Gymnastic work did not interest me and the simplest exercises made me ache all over. I heard that my case was quoted for years by Dr. Enebuska as encouragement of students who were not strong. But I persevered. As everyone knows, Swedish Gymnastics begin with simple fundamental work, progressing with combinations of these and more complicated exercises. After five minutes of standing erect I had to lie flat on three stools. After three months, however, I began to feel that I was better, and at the end of the year was doing all the gymnastics required. The second year Miss Homans sent me twice a week to Andover, where I taught the theory and practice of gymnastics to a class of teachers from the primary grades to the headmaster. . . . It is impossible to tell how my life had altered. I had changed an aching body to a free and strong mechanism, ready and eager for whatever might come. My indifference had changed to deep conviction and I wanted to work only in physical education so that I might help others as I had been helped.

---

[37] *Ibid.,* p. 659.

Of course part of Senda Berenson's "inspired teaching" came from the sort of person she was, and that, in part, came from her privileged background. The family were prominent in educational and cultural circles of New England. One sister became a sculptor, her brother a well-known art critic, and another sister married Ralph Barton Perry of the Harvard faculty. Senda herself in 1911 married Herbert Vaughan Abbott, professor of English at Smith, and son of the Reverend Lyman Abbott of Plymouth Church in Brooklyn.

In the beginning of her work at Smith it took everything she had to make headway. Finally the prestige, charm, courage, and determination of this young teacher did develop respect among her conservative colleagues for a new and nonacademic field. Senda Berenson was accepted as one of them, and accorded the dignity of marching with the full professors

**Senda Berenson, at the time of her graduation**

*Department of Hygiene and Physical Edu. Wellesley College*

in the academic procession! The students, on the other hand, were easy converts to her teaching, especially after she introduced basketball. Soon after James Naismith of nearby Springfield College invented basketball, Miss Berenson read an account of it, saw its possibilities, and tried it out at Smith. After experimenting with this vigorous game, and modifying the rules to suit her students she wrote an article "Basketball for Women." [38] It expresses so well her own ideas and policies that much of it is quoted below:

> The value of athletic sports for men is not questioned. It is a different matter, however, when we speak of athletics for women. Until very recent years, the so-called ideal woman was a small waisted, small footed, small brained damsel who prided herself on her delicate health, who thought fainting interesting, and hysterics fascinating. The fainting, hysterical maiden is now treated as a nervous patient, and in her place is that glowing, happy creature who advocates "mens sana in corpore sano." She does not go into athletics to outdo nor imitate her brother as some would have us believe. She does not run the danger of having professionalism creep into her athletics. She realizes more and more that by developing her body by as scientific and thorough means as her mind—making the former a means for the latter— she reaches the highest development of true womanhood.

She goes on to say that women have long felt the need of some sport that would give both physical development and enjoyment. Basketball fills this need since it requires action of every part of the body, and also physical courage, self-reliance, quickness and alertness. She then describes how the revised rules control roughness, and the division of the field encourages teamwork. After a description of lead-up plays and practice methods she again emphasizes the values of basketball:

---

[38] Senda Berenson, "Basketball for Women," *Physical Education*, 3 (September 1894), pp. 106–9. By permission.

Department of Physical Edu. Smith College

Modern basketball: an interclass game

159

It is a splendid game to develop physical courage. Timid students who are afraid to jump a low rope, who say with a pale smile that they are not made for athletics—meaning anything in the world except making a ball of themselves over a book—get so interested that before they know it they are in the midst of the runners. It also cultivates self-denial, as it teaches to give up one's own honors for the good of the whole, and gives good opportunities for self-control and gentle manners, all of which form such a great part in the development of character and true womanhood.

Rapidly the game spread to other colleges, and the rules began to vary. In 1899 a committee to draw up rules was appointed at a Springfield conference on physical training. The Boston Normal School of Gymnastics, Oberlin, Radcliffe, and Smith were the colleges represented, and Senda Berenson was appointed chairman. She edited the first Basketball Guide in 1901, and continued to do so until 1916–17.

Meanwhile other sports were introduced at Smith, and a college athletic association open to all students was officially recognized. In 1897 Miss Berenson went to Stockholm for four months' work at the Royal Central Gymnastic Institute. Here she took Swedish gymnastics, in which she had been well grounded at BNSG, and also fencing, under the direction of one of the fencing masters of the Swedish army.

Back at the college she began the interclass competitive demonstration of gymnastics—marching, floor work, and apparatus—that became the high point of the indoor season for Smith College women for years. Not only participants but all the rest of the college were interested to see which class would win the coveted Clarke cup, first awarded in 1900.

A new golf course at the edge of town was laid out as a joint project of college and community. Volleyball, tennis, fencing, archery, baseball and even cricket were added to the program. And then "One red letter day in 1901 Miss Applebee came to teach hockey. . . . Five hundred Smith girls in long skirts and high-necked shirtwaists literally fell at her feet." [39]

After her marriage in 1911, Mrs. Abbott resigned her position at the college, but continued to teach physical education part time at the Burnham School in Northampton. Her influence on college physical education and women's sports persisted: [40]

> Years have passed since she left the college, but there is scarcely a feature of the physical education programs of today, either at Smith or at many other colleges which cannot be traced back to some precedent set by her. . . . When students, alumnae, and friends of the college pass down Berenson Place, the broad approach to Scott Gymnasium which is the heart of the physical education department, they will be reminded that the place is fittingly so named for truly it was Senda Berenson and no other who led the way.

### Constance M. K. Applebee (1873–   ) Pioneer in women's sports: Field Hockey

No one recalls what the score was. The score didn't matter in that hockey match. No one recalls who all the men and women players were. It was 1901 and summer time. Outside the Harvard gymnasium a crude field was laid out. Each player was given a shinny stick.

Dr. Dudley Sargent, shinny stick in hand, stood where the coach said to stand. Dr. Tait McKenzie did too. Miss Harriet Ballantine, then director of physical education at Vassar College, took her place. Nineteen unknown others did likewise.

The coach—Miss Constance Applebee of England, later known affectionately to American hockey players as "The Apple" —placed a soft ball on the fifty-yard line. The whistle blew, and the first American field hockey match was on.[41]

---

[39] *Research Quarterly, op.cit.,* p. 664.
[40] *Research Quarterly, op.cit.,* p. 665.
[41] National Section on Women's Athletics, *Sports Bulletin* (November 1947), p. 1. By permission.

One could add, knowing Miss Applebee's ready humor, "and a good time was had by all." Miss Ballantine asked Miss Applebee to remain in this country and introduce hockey to students at Vassar. Other Eastern colleges wanted her help, so she brought the game to Bryn Mawr, Vassar, Wellesley, Smith, Mt. Holyoke, Radcliffe, and the Boston Normal School of Gymnastics. In 1904 she joined the faculty at Bryn Mawr and remained there until her retirement in 1928.

Soon a vigorous and varied sports program was in swing under her direction. It drew an amazing number of participants for a comparatively small student body. Some twenty-five class teams in hockey, and fifty teams in basketball were included in intramural competition. This was in addition to other sports such as swimming, water polo, track, tennis, fencing, archery, and badminton. Her influence developed high standards of sportsmanship.[43]

> They played . . . with all their hearts. To well-deserved victory or to defeat, each team fought to the last goal, played to the last whistle, and found satisfaction in having done their best. The team that had done its best could depend on Miss Applebee's praise regardless of the results of the game. Here "play for play's sake" did not disregard the vital fact that we play games to test our strength and skill against the strength and skill of others. Fairness was taken for granted, but the administration of it as exemplified in umpiring, was a matter of the strictest training and standards. Every interclass game was not only refereed by Miss Applebee or another instructor, but was umpired by four students, the captains and managers of the two classes not playing in the match.

Miss Applebee's interests and services on the Bryn Mawr campus went beyond sports. She directed the annual May Day festival; she helped students establish the *College News,* a campus paper. Her religious convictions took the practical

---

[43] *Research Quarterly, op.cit.,* p. 697.

turn of reconciling two rival organizations that were wasting their energy in competitive activities, and helping them form a united Christian Association.

Similarly, her interest and influence in field hockey went out beyond the Bryn Mawr campus and became nation-wide. In 1922 she helped to organize the United States Field Hockey Association, which she has supported actively since that time. In the same year she began and has since directed the September Hockey and LaCrosse camp at Mt. Pocono. During its many successful seasons literally thousands of school, college, and club players, as well as school and college teachers have profited by the expert coaching of "the Apple" and her staff. Moreover, they have appreciated and remembered the amusing "punch lines" of her instruction: [44]

> There was always a lecture that first evening at Hockey Camp. "The Apple" explained the rules of the camp. "Down there," she'd point, "there's a lake. You'll want to go swimming. I know you physical education teachers will be using that silly buddy system. I don't use it. I say you are to go in three's. Then there is one to drown, one to look on, and one to run tell about it." We went in three's. . . .

To the more mature and thoughtful campers, the example of vitality, enthusiasm, directness, and age-defying "hustle" has been as valuable as it was fascinating at the time. "The Apple's" quips have become legend, her tips on play are still astute hockey lore. Because of her work and her influence, field hockey has remained a players' game, satisfying the vigorous woman's wish to be part of a skilled, smart, demanding team— team-steered toward winning, team-disciplined in playing fair.

It was fortunate for the future development of women's athletics that the pioneers who introduced them were persons like Senda Berenson and Constance Applebee, interested in the

---

[44] National Section on Women's Athletics, *op.cit.*, p. 2.

sports they were teaching primarily as a fine experience for the players. Like Amy Morris Homans they had far vision and could foresee the stadium type growth of sports as a business, if not kept, as intramurals, an integral part of the college program. Since the early days, trained women teachers of physical education have consistently been alert both to the values of

Department of Hygiene and Physical Edu. Wellesley College

**Field Hockey is played after college**

controlled competition and the dangers of wild-cat promotion of women's sports as commercial spectacles.

The six women whose careers have been described in this chapter have greatly influenced our professional lives through their work. What characteristics gave them this long reach into the future?

1. Each saw a high purpose in her work, a purpose to be followed with tremendous drive.

2. Abundant energy made this drive possible. The energy came from sound physical health in most cases, but also from the mental health and emotional stability that an organized life evidences. It is interesting to note that they were long-lived.

3. They were deeply religious, seeking in their faith guidance for meeting problems, strength and balance for daily living.

4. Each was outgoing in relations with colleagues and students, gifted with the traits of personality that drew others along with her, both in work and in friendship.

5. They had high standards of excellence, applied first of all to their own work, also to the work of others.

6. Yet they were modest; demanding more of themselves than of others, they were more ready to give than anxious to receive the accolade for accomplishment.

7. With them human needs came first. In their time women's needs seemed paramount: women's health, women's freedom from limiting social customs and restricting dress, freedom to enter sports and other vigorous activities.

8. These were intelligent women, gifted with ability far beyond the average. Some writers distinguish between "academic" intelligence, or the ability to master and use knowledge, and "social" intelligence, or the ability to respond effectively in human situations. They demonstrated both types of intelligence.

9. Thus it is apparent that they were real as well as status leaders. The distinction is clear. A status leader is one who occupies a position of authority. A real leader is one who moves toward a goal and takes others with him. Status they had, but were not content to rest on it. By great effort they moved toward achievement.

The exceptional quality of these six women, including Catherine Beecher, not only stimulated the growth of physical education for women, but gave our profession status, dignity, and direction.

## QUESTIONS

1. Why was there no physical education in colonial schools?

2. Would you expect to find the difference mentioned between New England, the Middle Atlantic states, and the South in tolerance of amusements? Why?

3. What purpose did most leaders see in physical education up to World War I?

4. Do you know of any schools in which German or Swedish gymnastics are taught today?

5. Will it be any advantage to you as a physical education teacher to have the right to vote? Explain your answer.

6. Did your hygiene books in elementary or high school have material on the health effects of the use of tobacco and alcohol? What was the influence of this instruction?

7. What was the mean lifespan of the pioneers described in this chapter? Can you find out how this compared with the mean for all women at that time?

8. Review the qualities of a successful teacher of physical education as discussed in Chapter 2. Which of these were shown in the lives of the women discussed in this chapter? Did they have some not mentioned in Chapter 2? Did they lack some?

9. Select one of the women described in this chapter, and discuss what contribution her work makes to yours, as a student and, later, a teacher of physical education. Write a brief paper on this topic.

## SELECTED REFERENCES

AAHPER, *Supplement to Research Quarterly,* **12,** No. 3 (October 1941).

Ainsworth, Dorothy. *History of Physical Education in Colleges for Women* (New York: Barnes, 1930).

Cozens, F. W., and Florence Stumpf. *Sports in American Life* (Chicago: University of Chicago Press, 1953), Chaps. II, III.

Rice, Emmett A., J. L. Hutchinson, and Mabel Lee. *Brief History of Physical Education* 4th ed. (New York: Ronald, 1958), Chap. 22–23.

Van Dalen, Deobald, Elmer Mitchell, and Bruce Bennett. *A World History of Physical Education* (Englewood Cliffs: Prentice-Hall, 1953), Chap. XXII, XXIII, XXIV.

Weaver, Robert B. *Sports and Amusement in American Life* (Chicago: University of Chicago Press, 1939).

# CHAPTER 7

# Growth of Our Profession: 1914-1960

ANY GROUP OR NATION, threatened by danger, must look to its defenses. Man power, in terms of the health, strength, and skill of its people, is perhaps the first defense. So it is to be expected that the danger of war emphasizes the importance of physical education. Correspondingly, at such a time teachers of physical education tend to put war aims first, to consider health, strength, and skill as the most important purposes of their work. Since 1914 the United States has fought in two world wars, and has for more than fifteen years been engaged in a "cold war" with Communism. Moreover, a severe depression between the two wars has been succeeded by a spiraling inflation since the second war. Changes in our society and in the complexity of the problems we face have been so rapid, so confusing, that the period prior to 1914 seems, as Roy Baldridge once called it, "an age of incredible innocence." It is to be expected that changes in the ideology and in the practice of our profession have been correspondingly complex. In this chapter we shall summarize briefly some of these changes, both in physical education and in the status of women, illustrating them with biographical sketches of the other selected pioneers.

## Physical education in the United States from 1914–1960

The impact of World War I on physical education was felt even before this country declared war in the spring of 1917. Legislation requiring physical education in the public schools was passed in eight additional states from 1914 to 1918, in seventeen states from 1919 to 1921, in seven from 1922 to 1931, and in two since that time. Many states revised earlier laws to make them more effective. State directors were appointed in New York and California in 1916 and 1917, and this practice was followed by other states. At the present time more than forty states have designated a supervisor in this field, and states in which this person is trained for the job and working full time in the interests of health, physical education, and recreation, have improved those programs markedly.

When the United States entered the war there was much pressure to have military training substituted for the highschool boys' physical education program. While in some high schools and many colleges this was done, leaders in our profession (Thomas Wood, R. Tait McKenzie, Clark Hetherington, and others) as well as Secretary of War Newton D. Baker advised against the practice. Finally it came to be recognized that a vigorous high-school physical education program actually made better preparation for later military training, as well as for peace time living.

The armed forces called many men prominent in physical education and athletics to develop the army's physical training program. Joseph Raycroft, Walter Camp, John L. Griffith in this country, James McCurdy, James Naismith, and George

Meylan in France, and R. Tait McKenzie in England were among the many who did this work. Physical education men of draft age often served locally in base camps, or with the Y.M.C.A. overseas in leave areas. Women teachers of physical education made their direct contribution to the war chiefly through physical therapy, rehabilitation, and postwar relief in war areas.

After the war the military emphasis declined sharply, and a broader ideology brought in a more modern program. New concepts of education based on research in child study and psychology appeared in the writings of G. Stanley Hall, John Dewey, Edward Thorndike, William Kilpatrick, and others. Leaders in physical education also advocated changes. The emphasis in education now stressed how the child actually does learn, not how we think we ought to learn. He learns, said the experts, through his own efforts (by doing) to achieve his own goals (purposes and interests) and at his own rate (individuals differ). This meant a beginning of "child-centered" rather than "subject-centered" education. In physical education Thomas Wood, Clark Hetherington, and Rosalind Cassidy wrote about the "New Physical Education," and J. F. Williams and J. B. Nash continued to spread revolutionary ideas. Formal gymnastics, they said, are alien to the child's interests, give him little opportunity to learn, and have no desirable outcomes beyond exercise. On the other hand a "natural" program of sports, play, and dance will fit with the child's interests and so enlist his real effort. In addition he will have the opportunity to learn culturally valuable skills and as much or more exercise as in gymnastics, or so the theorists declared. Williams' article "Interest and Effort in Physical Education" [1] was followed by his useful series of texts in the field. Nash, in his many writings, interpreted, clarified and expanded Hetherington's concept of

---

[1] *American Physical Education Review* (September 1923).

the four levels of learning. Calling them the organic, neuro-muscular, cortical-interpretive, and emotional-impulsive, he discussed the contributions of our field to education at each level.

Meanwhile, in 1918, the National Education Association's Commission on Secondary Education produced its "Seven Cardinal Principles of Education": health, mastery of common tools, worthy home membership, vocational effectiveness, citizenship, worthy use of leisure, and character. Analyzing the contribution of physical education to these objectives emphasized our relationship to health education on the one hand, and to recreation on the other.

The depression of the thirties cut school expenditures to the bone. First to feel the cuts were the so-called special subjects. However, when the move to go "back to the three R's" took physical education out of the curriculum in some schools, pressure from the community restored it before very long.[2]

During the early decades of the century many lines of research in different disciplines were establishing holistic theories. The concept that the organism responds as a whole to the total situation was readily applied to physical education. It brought to our theorists the realization that a child thinks and feels, in a game, even as he runs. Moreover, thinking, feeling, and running all modify each other—or intensify each other, as the case may be. Therefore any physical education activity should be planned and taught with care for the emotional and social outcomes, as well as for skill and exercise. We began to hear the slogan "education *through* the physical, not *of* the physical." We also began to hear about integration as basic to mental health. The tendency to consider functioning wholes was apparent in the 1938 statement of objectives by the NEA.[3]

---

[2] Parents, children, and organizations; the American Legion, and the CIO.

[3] Educational Policies Commission, *The Purposes of Education in American Democracy* (Washington: NEA, 1938).

These were not stated as separate traits, but as the way we hope educated persons may act in four facets of living. Self-realization pictures the person as a well-developed individual; human relationships describes his behavior toward others; economic efficiency points out his competence as an earner and consumer; and civic responsibility shows his job as a citizen of a democracy in a free world. Again our relations with health and recreation were emphasized, i.e., the educated person protects his own health and that of his dependents; the educated person is participant and spectator in many sports and other pastimes.

The growing threat of totalitarianism brought home to us the need of clarifying our democratic values. Over the years we have become concerned to teach not only the values, but objectives, procedures and behavior that will make the values real. When the AAHPER was ready to publish its first yearbook, in 1951, it was a development of this theme.[4]

Thus our purposes in physical education grew beyond the uncomplicated prewar belief in exercise for health and strength. We added recreation, democratic human relations, and the integration of the whole child. Most writers in our field agreed that all of these were important, but there were differences in emphasis. To ask what is the most important purpose of physical education was to start a lively discussion in any professional group—the same question still gets the same response.

The differences were sharpened when the threat of totalitarian attack became a reality. World War II again emphasized the need for man power. The draft examinations shocked us because 40 per cent of the young men to be taken into the army were found unfit. The figure apparently was about the same as that of 1917. Had there been no improvement in the twenty-five years between? This question split our profession down the

---

[4] *Developing Democratic Human Relations through Health, Physical Education and Recreation*, First Yearbook (Washington: AAHPER, 1951).

middle. "We've been neglecting our main job" declared the mass-calisthenics advocates. "We can't be held responsible for poor teeth and psychoneurosis" declared the other camp— "moreover, we have long since graduated from the rank of drill master to the position of educator."

The armed services entered the argument. They, of course, set winning the war as their only objective. Their base camps set up strenuous fitness programs, and when they found our high-school graduates lacking in the strength and endurance to "take" these programs, there were emphatic complaints about school physical education. When women entered the services, chiefly in the WACS (army), WAVES (navy), and SPARS (coast guard), the question again arose. There was no doubt that they needed health, strength, and endurance on the job, although it was not the same degree needed by the men for combat duty. The WACS adopted an over-all "You must be Fit" program, and published a booklet under that title for the use of special officers as well as enlisted women. Their program was mass drill, and results were checked every three months by a "fitness rating test": dips, situps, wing lifts, and squat thrusts. This program was accepted at the height of war training, but during demobilization it was discontinued because of objections from enlisted personnel and company command-ers, in favor of a daily hour in physical recreation.[5] The WAVES and the SPARS left the problem to commanding of-ficers and their special officers at different bases. Consequently there were different types of programs, and much more time given to sports and athletics than in the original WAC pro-gram.

After the war the broader program in physical education gained new validity from studies of child development. It be-came apparent that, since children develop as unified organ-

---

[5] Mattie E. Treadwell, *U.S. Army in World War II Special Studies The Women's Army Corps* (Washington: Office of U.S. Army, 1954), p. 665.

isms, we must look at physical growth and improvement in motor skill in relation to increasing emotional maturity and social adjustment. Moreover, each child has his own pattern of growth; although they all go through a similar sequence, the rate of individual change differs. Therefore age-grade standards of achievement apply only in a limited way. Much more useful is the cumulative record of the individual child. One of the recent definitions of physical education emphasizes this point of view: "Physical education is the use of vigorous activity as planned developmental experience." [6]

Aside from changes in the purposes and objectives of our field, and corresponding changes in program, perhaps the most important development of the last forty-five years has been the increase in scientific study. Not only have individual leaders carried on research, but Universities have set up graduate programs leading to advanced degrees. In 1924, eight institutions offered a Master's degree in physical education, and two a doctorate in the field. By 1954 these numbers had increased to 158 and 36 respectively.[7] Our national organization began publishing the *Research Quarterly* in 1930, and has since put out useful books related to research. Scientific study depends on accurate instruments for measurement; there are now good texts in the field of measurement and evaluation of physical education. The AAHPER has sections on measurement and on research; there exists, as well, an affiliated research council.

The growth of our national organization is even greater than that of most professional groups allied with it.[8] All have contributed to promotion and to raising professional standards in the field. There are now more than 22,000 members of the AAHPER in comparison with a few thousand in 1914.

---

[6] Elizabeth Halsey and Lorena Porter, *op.cit.,* p. 2 and Chap. II.

[7] Harry Scott and Raymond Snyder, *Professional Preparation in Health, Physical Education and Recreation* (New York: McGraw-Hill, 1954), p. 37. Also Department of Health, Education, and Welfare, *op.cit.,* p. 3.

[8] A list of affiliated organizations is published on the organization page of each journal.

The status of physical education in our schools and colleges has improved very much since 1914. It is now generally accepted as a part of the required curriculum. During such periods of retrenchments as the depression there have been some cuts, and there are currently a few attacks in colleges. What has been called "sputnik fever" led to a general reappraisal of college and high-school programs in search of more time for mathematics and science. In some cases this was sought at the expense of physical education and other so-called special subjects. In some cities the public schools have seen a "back to the three R's" movement as part of the taxpayers' drive to economy. Although we are in a period of inflationary prosperity, there is the same popular argument against "fads and frills" in the school program that there was during the depression. This tends to emphasize the fitness objective of physical education and to minimize other less readily understood purposes.[9] However, the importance of our work has been placed on a sound foundation over a century of progress, and evidence in its support has been collected and made available by our national organization. If the public is kept informed of what we are doing in any situation, we do not need to fear lasting drastic cuts in the support of a good program.

Since World War I the growth of athletic sports has been phenomenal. Men's athletics have become a business grossing millions in football gate receipts. These sums have paid the way for travel, equipment, coaches' salaries, and other expenses of the so-called minor sports, which cannot support themselves by admission fees. The size and influence of the athletic budget is a constant problem in colleges and universities. "Money talks" as Coach Yost of Michigan once said; [10] money depends on having a winning team—and that depends on many strictly nonacademic factors. The argument that intercollegiate

[9] See Chap. 8, p. 217.
[10] In a conversation with the author in 1929.

and interscholastic athletics may provide sound educational experiences leads to the logical conclusion that they might well be supported as other educational experiences are supported, i.e., from the general budget of the school or college.

Since 1914 women's sports also have grown in numbers participating and in variety of activities. Paid attendance at games has not been a problem in most situations. From time to time pressure has been brought on schools, colleges, recreation systems, and unattached groups of players to go commercial, that is, to develop highly competitive programs that might attract a gate. But women's organizations as well as most men's have worked consistently to keep us amateur in spirit as well as in fact.[11] The present authoritative source of official rules and standards is the Division of Girls' and Women's Sports of the AAHPER. The division had its beginnings as a committee on women's athletics, appointed in 1917 by Dr. Burdick, then president of the American Physical Education Association. The purpose stated in the appointment of the committee was to codify official rules for sports, and to set standards of play. Ten years later the committee became the Women's Athletic Section of the APEA. Since that time it has grown in the complexity of its organization and the scope of its national influence in promoting sports on an amateur, game-for-the-player basis, whether intramural or extramural in form. From 1923 to 1940 another group very influential in its work was the Women's Division of the National Amateur Athletic Federation, counterpart of the men's division that had been formed earlier. The women's division was organized under the chairmanship of Mrs. Herbert Hoover. Membership in the women's division was by individuals and by groups: schools, colleges, and organizations that gave financial support and sub-

---

[11] Notably the coordinated program of the National Association for Physical Education of College Women, the Division of Girls and Women's Sports of the AAHPER, and Athletic and Recreation Federation of College Women.

scribed to the platform of standards. As their parallel efforts became identical, these two women's groups merged in 1940 as the National Section on Women's Athletics of the AAHPER.[12]

Dance is another part of the physical education program that has come to play an important role in the past fifty years. There were beginnings, of course, before 1914, but the great interest in folk dancing gathered momentum in the decade after the war. Elizabeth Burchenal promoted this interest, not only through work with community agencies, but also through her many books describing folk dances of various countries. Since that time square dance has had a spectacular revival both in schools and in community groups. The elementary school has come to use national dance as an aid to understanding our own culture at different periods and other cultures as well. Of great assistance to this understanding is the work of Dudley Ashton who has contributed a scholarly study on the ethnological approach to regional dance.[13] Modern dance has a unique place in the physical education program that has developed since 1914. It is described later in this chapter in connection with the biographical sketch of Margaret H'Doubler. It is enough to say here that whether it is called modern, contemporary, or creative dance it has a secure place in the curriculum of the modern college and high school; its principles have been well-adapted to elementary-school activities in dance, rhythms, and movement exploration.

An organization that has had great influence in promoting both sports and dance on an educational basis is the National Association for Physical Education of College Women. Founded in 1924 as a small group of women administrators

---

[12] Organizations change their names as their functions change, not merely to confuse later students of their history. Thus the APEA became the AAHPE in 1939, and the AAHPER in 1940. The WAS became the NSWA in 1940, and the DGWS in 1957, always keeping its relationship to the parent organization. See Appendix A, p. 249.

[13] Dudley Ashton, *An Ethnological Approach to Regional Dance* (State University of Iowa Ph.D. Dissertation, 1953).

of college departments, it has expanded its membership to include all department personnel, and expanded the scope of its work in response to the rapid social changes of our times. It is now a part of co-ordinated programs of research and planning carried on by eleven related groups.

Health education has become much more effective since 1914. Then it was a program of inspection and medical examination with the beginnings of some teaching. Today it is a broad program of healthful school living. Included are all factors that affect the child's health: the sanitary condition of the school plant, the healthful balance of work, rest, exercise and food during the school day, medical service to correct defects as well as to prevent exposure to disease, a cheerful and friendly social climate that will favor mental health, and instruction that will encourage the child to care for his own health and safety as well as that of others. College health departments have also broadened their programs, giving much more complete examinations to working personnel and to food handlers, as well as to students. In many institutions medical service includes infirmary care and health counseling, as well as house and office calls. In addition to general courses in hygiene, curricula for the training of teachers have been adopted to meet the growing demand for teachers and other personnel trained in personal and community health.

Many agencies in addition to the school have worked to improve health: the federal government's Department of Health, Education, and Welfare, state and city departments of health, the family, private agencies such as the Rockefeller and Kellogg foundations, professional groups such as the American Medical Association, the American School Health Association, the AAHPER and others. Representatives from various health promoting groups have come together from time to time to coordinate their efforts: the White House Conferences of 1930, 1950, and 1960, the National Conference for Co-operation in School Health in 1940, illustrate this trend.

Community recreation was stimulated in many ways by World War I. School buildings were used for various war efforts and increasingly for community recreation. The Playground and Recreation Association aided many communities in getting support for their recreation programs. During the twenties the number of recreation leaders doubled, and expenditures for recreation grew accordingly. The decade of the thirties saw an immediate cut in local programs.[14] However, after 1933 the recreation movement was developed by federal projects designed to put unemployed persons to work. The Work Projects Administration trained recreation leaders and cooperated with local communities in stimulating local programs. The Public Works Administration, moving more slowly, built local recreation facilities; and other New Deal agencies helped in various types of recreation area development—the National Youth Administration, the Civilian Conservation Corps, and others. The net result was to push the recreation movement well ahead of its normal expectation of growth.[15] During World War II recreation became firmly established as a government responsibility, both in military and civilian centers. Private agencies reenforced government recreation projects, notably the United Service Organization and the Red Cross. Meanwhile community recreation systems, compensating for loss of leaders to the armed forces, employed more women than ever before. At the close of the war there began an era of expansion in government recreation: communities, counties, states, and the federal government responded to popular demand by providing more facilities for a greater variety of activities. Private recreation agencies also increased their efforts and their offerings; commercial recreation found

---

[14] Halsey, op.cit., p. 211.

[15] According to estimates made by the National Recreation Association Field Representative in Chicago.

a developing market as per capita wealth increased. Training leaders for this growing field was undertaken by an increasing number of colleges and universities. In 1949, 40 institutions offered a major in recreation; by 1954 this number had increased to 98, as reported in Chapter 4.

## Status of women in the United States 1914–60

The Civil War made demands on women's time, mostly for volunteer work. Two world wars demanded their time also, but as paid workers filling gaps in the nation's manpower needs. The effect, of course, was to open job opportunities to them in great variety, and at good pay: [16]

> The First World War gave them skilled jobs in factories, and World War II offered women the first opportunity to work in assembly and inspection operations where it is said they revealed special aptitudes. For the first time in World War II women replaced men as welders, as riveters, and in innumerable kinds of skilled work on railroads, in shipyards, and in aircraft factories.
>
> Rallying to their country's need of utilizing all able bodied manpower, women were no longer discriminated against. If they worked, they were not forced into domestic and other service occupations. Employers, desperate for workers, hired and trained women for jobs that they would never before have considered women able to perform, and in each instance women demonstrated their capabilities and versatilities. As always in war periods, wages soared and women, no longer relegated to the lower paid jobs, found new and personally rewarding monetary reasons for working. After each war period a great many women withdrew immediately and returned to their homes; but never as many as were anticipated and particularly was this true in World War II.

---

[16] Ruby Joe Reeves Kennedy, "Women, Work, and Marriage." In typed Report of Symposium on Physical Education for Women in Modern Times. Hygiene and Physical Education Section of Wellesley College Alumnae Association, 1952.

Numerical confirmation of these statements may be found in the following table: [17]

### Table VI. WOMEN IN THE LABOR FORCE

| | Women Workers (14 years and over) | | |
| Year | Number | Percentage of all Workers | Percentage of all Women |
|---|---|---|---|
| 1900 (June) | 4,999,000 | 18 | 20 |
| 1920 (January) | 8,229,000 | 18 | 23 |
| 1930 (April) | 10,396,000 | 22 | 24 |
| 1940 (March) | 13,840,000 | 25 | 28 |
| 1945 (April) | 19,570,000 | 36 | 37 |
| 1947 (April) | 16,320,000 | 28 | 30 |
| 1958 (April) | 22,254,000 | 33 | 36 |

The type of work done has changed very much since 1870. In 1958 clerical workers were first, operatives second, service workers (except household) third, professional workers fourth, and private household workers fifth, in numbers of women workers. The picture within the professional group has changed. The largest section of them are teachers, but the percentage is 48 today in comparison with 90 in 1870. Today medical and health workers including nurses make up 26 per cent of the professional group, and the remaining 28 per cent are distributed among a great variety of callings: they are auditors, social workers, librarians, reporters, lawyers, musicians, and they even enter such unusual professions as engineering, architecture, geology, the ministry, and airplane navigation.[18] Among different age groups, older women have made the greatest gain in numbers employed. From 1940 to 1957 the percentage increase of married women between

[17] *1958 Handbook on Women Workers* (Washington: U.S. Department of Labor, Women's Bureau, 1958), p. 4.

[18] *Ibid.*, p. 13.

forty-five and sixty-four years in the labor force was 348, while the percentage increase in the population of the same group was only 43.[19] Why do these women work? According to Dr. Kennedy it is usually because they have to in order to support themselves and their dependents. A few work to buy a home, educate their children, or pay debts—a few because they love their jobs, but 84 per cent find it a matter of necessity.

That they can work as well as run their homes is due, of course, to the fact that it does not take as much time to do the latter job as it did in the early decades of the century. Labor saving appliances, prepared mixes and frozen foods, and outside services make the difference. Apparently these technological devices have not brought the relaxation of leisure for modern women, but have led to a complex of increasing activity. Child care in preschool years, a job when the children are older—or a full program of community work and social "obligations" make up the complex. All this is done in accord with the higher standards demanded by increasing information and sophistication. As Evelyn Whitman says of the homemaker's job: "We are not yet, in America, using labor-saving devices to decrease labor, but only to increase standards." [20]

The social revolution in women's lives came directly after World War I. The "roaring twenties" were years of disillusionment left after the crusading spirit of the war had quickly evaporated. "Flappers" scandalized their elders by bobbing their hair, using lipstick, shedding decorum at dances, rolling their hose, and wearing juvenile short-skirted, long-waisted dresses. All this has been called a search for lost youth. Certainly young men and young women together turned away from traditional concepts of duties and responsibilities in a determined search for gaiety. Then came the sobering years,

---

[19] *Ibid.*, p. 34.
[20] Evelyn Ardis Whitman, "I'm Tired of Grandma," in *Women Today* by Elizabeth Bragdon, ed. (Indianapolis: Bobbs-Merrill, 1953), p. 223.

the thirties. No one had money, no one could get a job. Married women were the first job casualties, but even single women were in difficulties. Social pleasures were less expensive, and the "dutch treat" concept of dating grew. Inexpensive clothing was adopted, and worn everywhere. Jeans and shorts were popular with men and women alike. World War II, as we have seen, multiplied jobs and put money in the pockets of women as well as men—money earned in the services, war industries, and civilian employment. Convention, as always in a society disturbed by war, seemed relatively unimportant, and almost any kind of recreation that did not require gasoline for driving was open to both sexes. Social freedom for women became an established fact. In recent years the balance of social responsibility has been restored by home training, increased attention to the meaning of religious teachings, and the individual's respect for the more durable conventions.

In 1914 women's civic and legal rights were still very limited. The vote was gained in 1920 after a sharp finale of dramatic struggle similar to the English battle, so well described by I. A. R. Wylie: [21]

> For two years of wild and sometimes dangerous adventure I worked and fought alongside vigorous, happy, well-adjusted women who laughed instead of tittering, who walked freely instead of teetering, who could outfast Gandhi and come out with a grin and a jest. I slept on hard floors between elderly duchesses, stout cooks, and young shopgirls. We were often tired, hurt, and frightened. But we were content as we had never been. We shared a joy of life that we had never known.

When the seventy years' effort had ended, leaders of the suffrage movement in the United States started the League of Women Voters, to help women become informed in the use of the ballot. Not only has this nation-wide, nonpartisan or-

---

[21] I. A. R. Wylie, "The Little Woman," in Bragdon, *op.cit.*, p. 21. By permission.

ganization grown from a handful to a membership of 128,000 women working in more than a thousand local leagues in all our states, but similar growth has been made by the public affairs divisions of many other women's organizations. Women cast about half the ballots in the 1956 presidential election, hold important party posts and elective offices, represent us abroad and in the United Nations.

Since they have had the vote, women's legal status has improved. In every state they are protected by standards controlling such working conditions as hours, wages, industrial home work, dangerous or unhealthful work, employment before and after childbirth, and plant facilities for health, safety, and sanitation. Many states have equal pay legislation, and the federal government has adopted this principle in its civil service regulations. Sixteen states and the District of Columbia require the same rate of pay for men and women teachers. Women are slightly favored in social security legislation since they are able to draw benefits at sixty-two instead of sixty-five. Single women have approximately the same contract and property rights as single men, and discrimination against married women in regard to these rights is gradually disappearing. It does, however, still appear in odd instances: [22]

> In South Carolina a bride whose trousseau was destroyed in a fire could not collect insurance, but her husband could, and did —and kept the money himself. In Michigan a court ruled that even the hair on a woman's head belongs to her husband, and he may sue for damages if a barber cuts it without his consent.

In all but six states parents have joint guardianship over their minor children; in dissolved marriages, custody of the children is determined by the courts in the interest of the children.[23]

Girls and young women have gone to school in increasing

---

[22] The *Denver Post,* June 18, 1959.
[23] *Spotlight on Women in the United States* (Washington: U.S. Department of Labor, Women's Bureau, 1957), pp. 39–45.

numbers. In 1957 over nine-tenths of boys and girls between
the ages of seven and seventeen were in school. After seventeen, however, enrollment decreased, more sharply for women
than for men: [24]

Table VII. SCHOOL ENROLLMENT AFTER SEVENTEEN

| Age | Percentage of Population in School | | | |
|-----|-----------|------|------|------|
| | *Female* | | *Male* | |
| | 1957 | 1950 | 1957 | 1950 |
| 18 and 19 years | 28 | 24 | 43 | 35 |
| 20–24 | 8 | 5 | 21 | 14 |
| 25–29 | 2 | — | 10 | 6 |
| 30–34 | 1 | — | 3 | 2 |

In 1910 women received 22 per cent of all college degrees conferred, in 1957 they received 34 per cent. However there is
only one woman out of nine candidates in the typical doctoral
procession, while one out of three in the M.A. group is a
woman. We have come a long way since the 1870's, when
press and pulpit both questioned the desirability of college
education for women. Now no one objects, but if the family
can afford to send only one child to college it is apt to be
the best qualified *boy*, not the best qualified child.

Young women in college have had much more interesting
opportunities in physical education. The programs have become more varied, with increasing emphasis on dance of various types, on coeducational classes in dance and individual
sports, and coeducational groups in the extracurricular program. Women leaders in the field have studied the changing
roles of women in our society and have seriously attempted
adaptations of our program to those changes.[25] Promising new

---

[24] *1958 Handbook on Women Workers, op.cit.,* p. 88.
[25] Notably the Wellesley Symposium of 1952, the CAPECW meeting
of 1957, and the Estes Park Conference of the DGWS and NAPECW in
1958.

developments will be discussed in the next chapter; pioneers in some of the more recent changes will be described in the remaining pages of this chapter.

## Ethel Perrin (1872–    ) Pioneer in school programs of physical education and health education

For years the public schools of Detroit have been the prototype of a modern and comprehensive program in physical education. This program was initiated in 1909 by Ethel Perrin. When the 1952 National Convention of the AAHPER was held in Detroit, much of the interest centered in this small person who had resigned as supervisor of physical education in the Detroit schools in 1923. In spite of this interim of almost thirty years, Ethel Perrin was well remembered and still held in affectionate regard by Detroit teachers, and, in fact, by many men and women among convention delegates from all over the country. At eighty years Miss Perrin showed the same warm charm and keen witted sparkle that had eased the way for her work and helped to spread her influence during her long professional life.

Ruth Murray, now head of the Women's Department of Physical Education at Wayne University, remembers that visit well. In honor of the occasion, Miss Perrin had her picture taken. "She looks lovely in the picture with that bright, alert, and charming gaze, and the delightful sense of humor she always had long ago when I, a novice teacher, used to see her directing the weekly meetings. . . . She was still very much interested in the program and personnel here and visited two or three schools, making telling comments on what she saw. Her gaiety and gallantry and her complete lack of any sense of self importance made a deep impression on me." [26]

When Miss Perrin came to Detroit she had already taught

---

[26] Personal communication from Ruth Murray.

Ethel Perrin at 80

for some years. She was an instructor at BNSG for fourteen years after her graduation in 1892, then one year at Smith and one at the University of Michigan filling in for the respective administrators on leave of absence. In 1908 she was asked to organize physical education for girls in the large Central High School in Detroit. The next year she was promoted to be supervisor in this field for the entire city system.

"She liked to tell of an incident that occurred as she was being interviewed for this supervisory position. One board member held out against a woman holding that position. Ethel was told that if she could persuade this man to vote for her the position would be hers. She met this gentleman with fear and trembling. He sat behind an enormous desk and glared at her, and said: 'Miss Perrin, just how long do you expect to give to each classroom in this program of yours?' Ethel, taken by surprise, blurted out 'Four and three-quarters minutes in each room.' Then the man said: 'Miss Perrin, I see you have put much thought into this—I shall vote for you.' Ethel now says that it took her some years before she realized he also was bluffing." [27]

At the start of her work there was not much of a place for physical education in the schools. Although Detroit was one of our larger cities, there were only three men and three women teachers of physical education to help the young supervisor. When she left to take another position after fourteen years, there were 350 special physical education teachers and fifteen supervisors. The program became full-sized when the platoon system of organizing the elementary-school schedule was set up in 1918, giving every child sixty minutes a day of physical education during school time, and plenty of after school athletics. At about this time "stunts," or as we now call them "self-testing activities" were introduced, and the squad system under student leadership was used to make this part of the work effective in large classes. Formal gymnastics, so much a part of Ethel Perrin's early training and teaching at BNSG, disappeared from the Detroit program as she became more conversant with new developments in educational psychology.

Because of Miss Perrin's great interest in health, the physical education department took over a new program in health education introduced by the school administration. "Forty teachers gave their whole attention to this phase of the program." This development influenced Ethel Perrin to attend a summer conference in the interest of health education at Lake Mohonk in 1922, and this led to her appointment, the next year, as the Associate Director of the Health Education Divi-

---

[27] Personal communication from Maude Vrooman.

sion of the American Child Health Organization. She describes her work:

> I spent thirteen delightful years in comradeship with educators from all fields having a common interest in making health a vital part of school programs. I traveled all over the country to interpret to those in the field of physical education where and how they fitted into the picture, and to stress to the general educator and to those interested in other phases of health, the importance and the place of physical education in an inclusive health program. I attended conferences, large and small, making contributions from the platform and in small group meetings. From the central office, I sent articles to magazines and newspapers through our publicity division, and I talked over the radio. I also had a large correspondence with classroom teachers who asked us for help. From the letters we learned the needs of teachers and we prepared our printed material and planned our conferences to meet these needs. Being a part of a national movement brought a new satisfaction, but a far less definite one than that which comes from seeing results from efforts focused in one locality. In 1936 the American Child Health Association closed its doors and the doors of my farm opened wide and have been open ever since.[28]

Miss Perrin was by nature a person with whom others liked to work. She served as president of the Midwest Society of Physical Education in 1917–18, and as vice-president of the APEA from 1920–23. She was also a member and chairman of the executive committee of the Women's Division of the NAAF. Her publications were widely used: the Course of Study for the Detroit schools, and the State Course of Study for Michigan were largely her work. She wrote for children *Health in Play* and *My Health Book* both published by the ACHO. She was one of the first (1931) group to receive the Honor Award of the APEA, and also was given its distin-

---

[28] *Research Quarterly, op.cit.,* p. 686.

guished Gulick Award in 1946. Her sustained enthusiasm is well expressed in her own words:

> My forty-four years of professional life were uninterrupted. My vacations grew shorter and shorter but my health never failed me nor did my spirit ever waver. To this I owe the great happiness from my work.[29]

### Lillian Curtis Drew (1873–1930) *Pioneer in individual gymnastics*

The health of her students was always a directing force in the teaching of Lillian Drew. She was a contemporary of Ethel Perrin and Senda Berenson—a year later than they in graduating from BNSG (1893). Like so many of Miss Homans' students, Lillian Drew had the advantages of a rich cultural home environment. Ancestors on both sides traced the past back to early colonial leadership. Parents brought lively interests of the day into family discussions of events, books, music, and religion. As a result her personality was illuminated by the many facets of her interests, and this in turn gave depth and breadth to her teaching.

Soon after her graduation from BNSG, Miss Drew began her specialization. She became an instructor of corrective gymnastics in the office of the well-known Boston orthopedists, Drs. Bradford and Brackett. Here she remained for fifteen years, absorbing valuable experience and training in the medical theory underlying her work, and testing in a practical way the results of individual exercises. Next she taught at Teachers' College in Columbia University from 1909–19, lecturing to professional students in physical education and to teachers who came to summer sessions from all

---

[29] *Ibid.*

over the country. Her subjects were the theory and practice of corrective gymnastics, kinesiology, anatomy, and physiology. During World War I she served as Supervisor of Reconstruction Aides for War Service, a post involving final interviews of all aide candidates and recommendations (or not) on the basis of personality and general fitness for the work. She also taught courses in physiotherapy, massage, and bandaging to other war personnel.

After the war Miss Drew joined the faculty of the Central School of Hygiene and Physical Education in New York, which had been founded in 1909 by Helen McKinstry, a prominent BNSG graduate.[30] For the next ten years she lectured there in individual gymnastics, massage, kinesiology, and anatomy. She also taught evening classes in the Central Y.W.C.A. to business women who needed both instruction in posture and relief from the strain of their work. Professional writing, offices in various organizations, consultant and even teaching service to various schools and universities in the New York area crowded her days and evenings, as she never spared herself. Her first book: *Individual Gymnastics,* was published in 1922; her second: *Adapted Group Gymnastics,* in 1927. In addition numerous magazine articles, radio talks, and movies were produced in these years. Development of the field of individual gymnastics was broadened as well as stimulated by her very sound, constructive work.

When she retired from the Central School in 1929, Lillian Drew had a multitude of plans for relaxation and leisure—plans never to be fulfilled. Death cut short her life in 1930, at the age of fifty-seven. Among the many tributes to her influence as a person and to her work as a teacher, two are of special interest: [31]

---

[30] At first housed in the Central Y.W.C.A. of New York, in 1930 the school became the Department of P.E. at Russell Sage College.

[31] Alumnae files, Mary Hemenway Hall, Wellesley College.

A year or so ago I heard some of Miss Drew's students speak of her as their favorite teacher, agreeing that first of all, she was a *person*. (Louise Freer)

. . . She was one who essentially appreciated the individual. To Miss Drew, as to others of open mind, the growing flexibility of method in physical and in all education in recent years, the far simpler, franker, and more effectual teacher-pupil relationship, the increasing recognition of the individual and of the need of growth and change in all essential educational method to keep pace with the changing nature of life itself, all this must have been a great satisfaction. (Ethel Perrin)

## *Dorothy Enderis (1880–1952) Pioneer in school-community recreation*

Students at the University of Iowa, when planning their annual "Career Conferences" in the postwar days, always wanted different speakers each year—with one exception. "Let's have Dorothy Enderis from Milwaukee for Recreation, there's no one like her." So for several years Dorothy Enderis visited us for two days, speaking to the group as a whole and counseling individual students who were interested in recreation leadership as a career. The students were right—there was no one like her. She was an unassuming speaker although definite and very wise. Humorous, with a humor free from cutting edge or questionable taste, she held the attention of her audience apparently without effort. Actually, the sound, well-organized substance was put forth with such directness and simplicity that it was arresting. The individual conferences were enjoyed both by Miss Enderis and the student. Every student was of interest to her, and treated as a person in her own right. This was an inherent part of Dorothy Enderis' nature; she exemplified the trait she looked for in her personnel:

There is a German word I have never been able to put into English—*leutselig*. *Leute* is the German word for people, and *selig* is holy; and to me the finest attribute with which you could credit a recreation worker is *leutselig,* meaning people are holy to him.[32]

Miss Enderis grew up in Milwaukee, attended the Milwaukee public schools and the Milwaukee Normal School. On graduating from the latter she studied library science at the University of Wisconsin and then served as librarian in the Milwaukee Normal School from 1901 to 1909. Then followed three years as a successful fourth grade teacher in the "Bloody Fifth" ward. Her experience in dealing with these underprivileged children opened her eyes to their need for a constructive after-school recreation program. When Milwaukee became the first city to operate under the Wisconsin law of 1911,[33] a new Extension Department in Charge of Community Recreation under the Board of Education was formed. Four teachers were designated as staff: Dorothy Enderis, L. H. Kottman, and Robert Witt, working under Harold O. Berg as director. They began a program in 1912, with two experimental social centers and plenty of opposition. As the program proved itself, the opposition changed to consistent support. On Mr. Berg's retirement in 1920, Miss Enderis was made director; this work she continued until her retirement in 1948. By 1948 there were 32 social centers, 62 playgrounds, and a varied year-round program. Milwaukee citizens could find, in the school centers, musical activities, such speech activities as drama and parliamentary practice, crafts and applied arts, dance of various kinds, and a great variety of seasonal sports. Her recommendation for 1949 called for a budget of $900,000, and a staff of 50 full-time and 1,200 part-time recreation workers. It was approved by the school board.[34]

---

[32] *Recreation* **46:**206, quoted in Lela B. Stephens "The Lady of the Lighted School House—Dorothy Enderis," (Delta Kappa Gamma, Milwaukee 1955), p. 12. By permission.

[33] Halsey, *op.cit.,* p. 187.

[34] Stephens, *op.cit.,* p. 10.

During these years of steady growth both in size and effectiveness of its recreation program, Milwaukee became known as the "City of the Lighted School House." It was visited by recreation authorities from other cities and from other countries as well. Not only did the program grow, it was flexible enough to change. It met the emergencies of the depression, of war service, of the thousand and one problems that come up whenever a city tries to cope with the social needs of its people. In this big job of administration, Dorothy Enderis did things in a big way: [35]

> She selected those who were to work for her very carefully, then she gave them a free hand. . . . She always managed to keep in touch with what was going on, and seemed to know just when a hearty laugh would relieve the tension which is bound to develop in any office. . . . (She was) one of those pleasant and comfortable people who, though being alert, never give the impression of being hurried. She had a way of accomplishing every detail and revolutionary things with the same matter-of-fact ease.

Milwaukee not only believed in and supported her work, it admired and loved Dorothy Enderis as a person. Evidence is plentiful: awards, citations, and honorary memberships in everything from the Junior League, the Phi Beta Kappa chapter of Downer college, to the Milwaukee Council of Consolidated Indian Tribes. There were also honorary degrees from neighboring Carroll and Lawrence Colleges, a citation for meritorious service from the University of Wisconsin, and national recognition from the AAHPER (Honor Award in 1942), the CBS (War Service Award in 1944) and the Office of Civil Defense (Merit Award 1945). As might be expected her own organizations gave her responsibilities: in Zonta, Delta Kappa Gamma, the Wisconsin Recreation Commission, and the Society of Recreation Workers of America she served

---

[35] Stephens, *op.cit.,* p. 16.

in numerous official capacities. The Federal Government needed her help for the Conference on Problems of Defense Areas (1941), Civilian Advisory Board for WAC (1943), and the National Committee on Social and Religious Activities for Servicemen (1948). This last committee was of special interest to Miss Enderis, closely allied as it was to her experience in social service and to her deep religious faith.

Dorothy Enderis wore all these honors lightly. Although she did the work involved with great seriousness, she never took herself seriously. When a thousand or more persons from Milwaukee and other cities gathered to honor her on the occasion of her retirement, there was an overwhelming deluge of praise and appreciation. That is, it would have overwhelmed most persons, but not Dorothy Enderis. At the end, when it was time for her response, she smiled her warm smile and remarked, calmly: "I have lived here all but the first year of my life, and have never met this woman you are talking about."

## Mabel Lee (1888–   ) Pioneer in professional organizations

Our national association has been unique in the fact that both men and women have shared the responsibility of planning and administration as well as the drudgery of committee work and detailed secretarial jobs. The list of presidents of the AAHPER includes a number of women; it has become the general policy of late years to alternate men and women in this position.[36] Doubtless the fine work of Mabel Lee, the first woman to be president, pointed up the fact that the job could be done equally well by qualified persons of either sex.

The list of Mabel Lee's professional accomplishments and recognitions is impressive. Probably the most significant is this presidency of our national organization, which at that time,

---

[36] Van Dalen, Mitchell, and Bennett, *op.cit.,* p. 484.

in 1931–32, was the American Association of Physical Education. Her indefatigable attention to detail as well as her powers of organization made it a very successful year from many viewpoints. With characteristic eagerness to offer guidance to others, Miss Lee composed a set of precedents, a calendar of duties that was really a step-by-step job analysis of the presidency. Executive officers of district associations as well as the national for many years found this "precedents" book very useful as a check list of things to be done.

Mable Lee grew up in Centerville, Iowa, and received the B.A. degree magna cum laude from Coe College in 1908. She then studied physical education at the BNSG with the class that had one year in Boston and one at Wellesley. After receiving the certificate from the latter college, she went back to Coe College as director and remained for eight years. Then came administrative positions at Oregon Agricultural College, Beloit College, and finally the University of Nebraska where she remained until her retirement in 1952. Summers took her first to the study of dance (Chalif in 1914, Vestoff-Serova in 1917) and then to teaching at Oneonta in 1922, the University of Texas in 1939, and the University of Southern California in 1952.

During these years of service to various institutions she wrote *The Conduct of Physical Education,* and, with Miriam Wagner, *Fundamentals of Body Mechanics,* as well as numerous articles. But it was in service to different organizations that Miss Lee did pioneer work. Not only was she the first woman to be president of the national association, but also the first woman president of the American Academy of Physical Education, in 1940. Her other honors include the annual Honor Award of the AAHPER in 1933, election to Academy membership, two honorary degrees, one from Coe College in 1939, and the other from George Williams College in 1957. She served on two important committees during World War II:

the Civilian Advisory Committee to the WAC,[37] and the Women's Division of Physical Fitness of the Federal Security Administration.

Since her retirement she has served as consultant in physical education to the Ministry of Iraq, under the Fullbright Act in 1952–53. She has been coauthor of the revised edition of Rice's *History of Physical Education,* published in 1958, and in 1957–58 received an Amy Morris Homans Fellowship to facilitate the writing of her memoirs. As chairman of the committee on the Seventy-fifth Anniversary, she contributed a great deal to the success of the Diamond Jubilee convention of the AAHPER, and edited the Anniversary number of the journal. She continues her committee work and speaking commitments, both to community and professional groups.

Among Miss Lee's students and colleagues are many devoted admirers. To them her attractive appearance and taste for dainty clothes as well as her very high standards of social conduct, professional excellence, and her indefatigable capacity for work, epitomize the desirable qualities of a leader in our field.

## Margaret H'Doubler Claxton (1889–    ) Pioneer in dance

On a winter afternoon in 1917, a radiantly enthusiastic young woman charged into a small office in Mary Hemenway Hall: "Liz, I've found it! Now, finally, I know where I'm going." Then came a torrent of words, describing dance and dance teaching: good, bad, and indifferent, as she had seen it in New York during the season. From all of these impressions Margaret H'Doubler was distilling her own clarified theory of what dance might mean. The rest of her professional life

---

[37] Miss Lee was of great assistance to Donna Niles and Dorothea Coleman in planning the WAC handbook *You Must Be Fit* and gave complete approval to the program of mass calisthenics and strength testing that characterized the WAC physical fitness program.

would be given to working out and to modifying this theory, to teaching hundreds of students at the University of Wisconsin and elsewhere significant communication through dance. As she saw it in 1917, dance must be freed from the old-time rigidity of the ballet, and, on the other hand, rescued from the formless individual interpretation of music by movement— any movement that occurred to the dancer at the time. Through continuous work in choreography, teaching, dancing, and study at Wisconsin, where she was a member of the physical education faculty, Margaret H'Doubler related dance to the arts of design, theater, and music. In 1919 her dance students became a production group, and the first Orchesis was formed. Later many honorary dance groups in other colleges adopted the name and the purpose. By 1926 Miss H'Doubler was ready to ask for a major program in dance. This was approved all the way up the academic line of authority, including the Board of Regents. It is reported that this *fait accompli* was finally discovered with a degree of astonishment, not to say incredulity, by certain representatives from rural areas in the state legislature. The program was the forerunner, by several years, of dance specialization in other universities. In 1925 Margaret H'Doubler published her magnum opus *Dance in Education,* followed by many articles and another substantial book in 1940: *Dance: A Creative Art Experience.*

Miss H'Doubler credits her career in dance to the initial suggestion and constant encouragement of Blanche M. Trilling, for many years head of the Department of Physical Education for Women at the University of Wisconsin. This is only one of several examples of Miss Trilling's wisdom as an administrator; of her ability to look ahead and forecast important developments in the field, and her almost uncanny success in selecting talented personnel and promoting their development.

When modern dance reached the concert stage, concert artists found hospitality and appreciation at Madison. Among them were Harold Kreutzberg, Doris Humphrey, Charles

Weidman, Martha Graham, Hanya Holm, and others. An artist to her fingertips, Miss H'Doubler had no room in her generous nature for the jealousy supposed to be characteristic of artistic temperament. She made every effort to secure other artists, both for concerts and for master lessons for her students. Thus the seasons' programs in dance were enriched, not only for University students, but for lay audiences in Madison. By the end of the year large and enthusiastic audiences were ready to see the final student programs.

Graduates of the dance major at Wisconsin have gone to teach in schools, colleges, universities, and a few to concert and theater work. Miss H'Doubler has been called to conduct workshops in more than a dozen places, here and abroad: in Canada, England, Luxemburg, and Sweden. She has been elected to honorary scholastic, dance, and physical education groups. Her happy marriage to Wayne Claxton, professor of art at Wayne University in Detroit, has not interfered with her career—nor with his. Since her retirement in 1953 she has been much in demand as guest teacher and lecturer.

The occasion of her retirement was marked by the alumnae as they thought "Margie H'Doubler" would like to have it marked. Professional talk interspersed with dance lessons brought together both past and present students, caught up again in the excitement of working with a creative artist. Margaret H'Doubler is an artist—in teaching, in choreography, in production. Above all, she is an artist in human relations.

### Dorothy Ainsworth (1894–    ) Pioneer in international relations

Transatlantic phone calls and cables are no rarity at the Northampton residence of Dr. Dorothy Ainsworth, formerly head of physical education at Smith College. They keep her in direct touch with various programs and projects of many international organizations, but especially with those of the

Dorothy Ainsworth

International Association for Physical Education of Girls and Women. This rapidly growing ten-year-old holds its fourth International Congress at the University of Maryland in August 1961. Dr. Ainsworth, like Mary Hemenway in the early Boston days, uses substantial private financial resources to stimulate and underwrite educational experiments that have claimed her interest.

Her interest in the international scene began when she went overseas with the Smith Motor Unit after World War I. From March 1919 to January 1920 she drove all over France carrying out assignments for the reconstruction program. Typical of her concern for persons is the fact that she still visits the village near Amiens that was headquarters in the postwar service days, and has kept contact with her friends in the village as well as with VIP's in Paris.[38] After this service to France, frequent visits abroad have kept Dr. Ainsworth in close touch with new professional developments and leaders in many other countries.

In the summer of 1927, Dorothy Ainsworth took a six-weeks' course in "primary gymnastics" with Nils Bukh at Hellerup, Denmark. In 1933 a sabbatical year gave opportunity for foreign study that included work with Rudolph Bode in Germany, Dalcroze in Hellerau, and Elizabeth Duncan (sister of the dancer Isadora) in Salzburg. Dr. Ainsworth also attended a meeting of the International Ling Society, later the International Society for Physical Culture. Meanwhile the idea of an international meeting in the interest of physical education for girls and women was brewing in the United States, suggested by Anna Hiss of the University of Texas, and strongly supported by Dorothy Ainsworth. It was given more definite form when the latter conferred in Copenhagen with Agnete Bertram, a leader in Danish Physical Education. Madame Bertram proposed that such a meeting be held in Copenhagen near the time of the Lingiad (national gymnastic festival of Sweden) of 1949. Each of the conferees took the idea to her own country and enlisted the financial support necessary to make the meeting possible. In the United States the NAPECW sponsored the project, in Denmark the government did so. Danish and American organizing committees went busily to work; the result was the first International Congress of Physical Education for Girls and Women, in Copenhagen, July 18–23, 1949. Attended by 235 delegates from 24 countries, the program was enthusiastically received, and a continuing committee appointed, with Dorothy Ainsworth as chairman. The general wish of delegates to have meetings

---

[38] Dorothy Ainsworth tells with obvious pleasure that the bright young daughter of her laundress, whose schooling in Amiens was financed by "American friends" derived so much prestige from this education that she eventually married the village butcher!

at three or four year intervals has been carried out: at Paris in 1953, London in 1957, and in the United States in 1961. A constitution was adopted at the London meeting, and a magazine, the *Review,* published twice a year, made its first appearance in the spring of 1958.

Meanwhile many other international projects and organizations have been initiated or supported by Dr. Ainsworth. For many years she served as chairman of the Joint Council of International Relations of the AAHPER, which co-ordinated the international work of all affiliated organizations, as well as the state chairmen of international relations serving under the AAHPER. The main purpose of this co-ordinated program was cultural interchange of persons and of ideas through visits, exchange of students and teachers, literature, correspondence, and meetings. Since the formation of a section on International Affairs of the AAHPER, the Joint Council is chiefly concerned with supplying the information to state chairmen that will help them with such local work as entertainment of foreign students and teachers, speakers, visitors, and arranging for them opportunities to meet their opposites in this country, and to see characteristic American events and institutions.

Dorothy Ainsworth has represented the AAHPER at many international meetings: in 1950 as president of our national organization, at the Pan American Congress of physical education in Uruguay, at the conferences of World Organizations of the Teaching Profession, and at the World Seminar in physical education, health, and recreation at the time of the Olympic Games in Helsinki.

In July 1959 a meeting of persons interested in health, physical education, and recreation, from many countries, was held in Washington prior to the annual conference of the World Confederation of Organizations of the Teaching Profession. This July meeting was organized by a subcommittee of the World Confederation, the committee on health, physical education, and recreation. It was attended by over 100 men and women from 36 different countries.[39] It was here decided to form an International Council on Health, Physical Education, and Recreation as part of the World Confederation structure. A petition for acceptance and a constitution were drawn up, and both were approved at the subsequent meeting of the parent organization (WCOTP). Dorothy Ainsworth was elected president of this important group.

When in Latin America in 1950, Dr. Ainsworth saw in action a dance group at the University of Brazil, and conceived the idea of arranging for them a goodwill tour of various schools and colleges in the United States. Local hospitality was to be provided by the host city, and a dance concert to be given at each stop by the group. It was the hopeful anticipation that travel expenses might be met by ticket sales for the various concerts, and travel to and from the United States was paid by the individuals in the group. This somewhat hazardous financial arrangement was underwritten by the author of the tour, which eventually covered a large section of the eastern seaboard and the Midwest. Certainly Dorothy Ainsworth's generous investment was amply repaid by the outcomes, both for the hosts—fascinated with the charm and voluble responsiveness of their guests; and the guests—high-spirited, wide-eyed, gaily absorbing new sights, sounds, and souvenirs.

Another colorful event of broader professional import was the Connecticut Valley Congress, an international meeting in the spring of 1954, held in connection with the national conference of the AAHPER in New York. Four colleges of the valley: Springfield, Smith, Holyoke, and Amherst, were host institutions, and the delegates saw each institution in turn as the program moved from one to another. The opening meeting at Smith was addressed by the U.S. Commissioner of Education,

---

[39] Dorothy Ainsworth, "The 1959 WCOTP Meeting," and "Our New International Role," *JHPER*, **30** (November 1959), pp. 17–21.

and speakers of international repute were heard at other sessions. These arrangements also were largely organized by Dr. Ainsworth as chairman of a committee representing the four colleges. Three hundred delegates from 41 countries were in attendance.

All of this activity in the interest of improving intercultural understanding has been carried on while a large department was being administered, and other professional offices were well-discharged. Dorothy Ainsworth was eighth in the line of women leaders who served as president of the AAHPER, in 1950–51. She has received the honor award of the association, and was elected to the American Academy. She has written the *History of Physical Education in Colleges for Women* in 1930; served as editor of *Individual Sports for Women* in 1949; and in 1955 collaborated with Ruth Evans to produce *Basic Rhythms*. To accomplish so much took a flair for organization, the ability to enlist the wholehearted co-operation of others, and, of course, her own great energy effectively directed. After Dr. Ainsworth's retirement from her administrative work at Smith in 1960, a dozen enterprises have held their place on her schedule, and a dozen new projects will fill it to overflowing, as always.

It is not very feasible to look for common characteristics of the six pioneers described in this chapter. They represented widely different lines of interest within our field, interests best served by very different temperaments. However, it is safe to say that they shared some traits with the pioneers described in Chapter 6. Each had the drive toward a strong purpose, and the energetic ability that made accomplishment of the purpose possible. To all twelve of these women the rest of us owe a great debt, as we do to the equally effective and dedicated men among the leaders of our profession. The women who demonstrated so clearly what physical education could mean to other women have left a legacy to you, and to me. It is a legacy of opportunity as well as of responsibility. We have the freedom to be active, fun-loving devotees of sports, dance, skills. We have the freedom to teach, to administer, to study, to experiment, to report our results so that we and others may be better teachers. Either homemaking or careers in our profession—or both—are open to us. It behooves us to ask ourselves if we can receive this fine legacy, develop it, and in turn leave an improved heritage to the next generation of teachers.

## QUESTIONS

1. Compare the effects of the two World Wars on physical education.

2. Compare the effects of the two World Wars on women's work, and on social conventions.

3. What was the effect of the depression on school physical education? On community recreation?

4. Which of the four general purposes of education as stated by the Educational Policies Commission in 1938 is of greatest concern to physical education? How does our work contribute to each of the four purposes?

5. Make a brief Who's Who of the persons mentioned in Chapters 6 and 7, not including the twelve pioneers; add to it names of other leaders in the field, both men and women.

6. Make a glossary of the unfamiliar terms found in the last two chapters.

7. In your opinion does the fact that one woman in three works for pay outside the home make any difference to those planning high-school programs in physical education? Explain.

8. What main objective was your high-school program in physical education planned to achieve? Can you think of ways in which it might have been improved?

9. List four opinions of physical education that you have heard expressed by different persons of your age or older; try to identify them with the era to which they belong, chronologically.

10. Interview some foreign student in your college to find out all you can about physical education in the schools of his country.

## SELECTED REFERENCES

Cozens, F. W., and Florence Stumpf. *Sports in American Life* (Chicago: University of Chicago Press, 1953), Chap. II, III.

*National Conference on Social Changes and Implications for Physical Education and Sports Programs* (Washington, D.C.: AAHPER, 1959), pp. 9–31, 59–66.

Rice, Emmett A., John L. Hutchinson, and Mabel Lee. *Brief History of Physical Education,* 4th ed. (New York: Ronald, 1958), Chap. XXII, XXIII, XXV, XXVI.

Sefton, Alice. *The Women's Division of the National Amateur Athletic Federation* (Stanford: Stanford University Press, 1941).

Van Dalen, Deobald Elmer Mitchell, and Bruce Bennett. *A World History of Physical Education* (Englewood Cliffs: Prentice-Hall, 1953), Chap. XXV.

Von Borries, Eline. *History and Functions of the National Section on Women's Athletics* (Washington, D.C.: NSWA, 1941).

# CHAPTER 8

# *Unfinished Business:*

## THE GROWTH OF OUR PROFESSION IN THE FUTURE

AFTER THE PUSH to the West Coast and the "Rush to the Rockies" it seemed as if this country had no more frontiers to be conquered. Adventure-loving Americans ever since, however, have found pioneering possibilities in a great number of directions: some scientific, some social and economic, and many, of necessity, political. In the midcentury decades the pace of change in our environment has been so rapid as to call for the boldest thinking and action to keep up with it. The scope of this thinking and action has become not national, not just international, but cosmic. No one knows just where our new frontiers are; no one doubts that strenuous efforts of exploration are ahead.

So it is in our profession: we have come the long way to reacceptance of physical education, to readoption of the classic Greek ideals of unity of body and mind, but much unfinished business is ahead. The two previous chapters have given an overview of the process in the United States through which physical education has become an established part of the modern school. This chapter will discuss remaining frontiers in our profession: problems that are critical today, reassessment of our basic values, and education for change.

## Understanding children and youth

For centuries and in different cultures we have worked with children and youth with a very creditable record of success. Always, however, we looked back on mistakes that have been made because we did not fully understand children as children, or adolescents as adolescents, but treated both as small adults. Meanwhile facts are at hand to correct this view —if we will but use them. Some of our own research personnel, as well as others in child welfare, education, psychology, and sociology, have been accumulating data that should be put together, reinterpreted, and applied to program-planning and to method in our field. We now know that children develop simultaneously along different lines that are closely related to each other. For example, we may analyze improvement in motor skills and social skills separately, but we realize that they occur at the same time and affect each other. So it is with emotional maturity, physical growth, and mental development. In other words we may have to divide a child for purposes of analytical research, but in teaching we should treat him as he is —an indivisible whole. This fact of wholeness tells us that when we teach games we should get desirable outcomes in the control of emotions, in getting along with others, in thinking up strategy, as well as in better skill and more exercise. We also know from analytical research that no two children develop at the same rate, or with the same balance between different lines of growth, although almost all go through the same sequence. Bill may be much larger than Tom but less skillful in throwing and catching and less mature in meeting obstacles without frustration. This fact of unique patterns tells us that it is better to keep individual cumulative records from year to year and evaluate the child's performance according to his own pattern of development than to set up age-grade standards with which all should be compared. In any one grade different children will need balls of different sizes, and turning bars at different heights: they should have free choice of equipment they wish to use. There remain many unsolved problems, not only in child growth but also in adolescent needs.

We need to know more definitely the sequence in which motor skills develop and the degree of variation from the sequence. We need practical studies to tell us what apparatus is most developmental for playground, gymnasium, and home yards. (Developmental apparatus not only provides plenty of exercise and use of arm and trunk muscles but also invites the invention of new ways to use the apparatus.) We need to know the sequence of social adjustment in play: when to introduce games with two sides; how to develop team feeling from the more amorphous "side" feeling; when to introduce relays to promote team feeling; methods of selecting more highly organized teams; length of time team personnel should play together; term of captaincy, and other conditions. We need to know the effect of different degrees of permissiveness in class situations on the kind of social outcomes. We need to know the differences in group pressures and group structures in different forms of physical education: dance, games, self-testing, movement exploration. We need to know the effect of these group relationships on the withdrawn as well as the overaggressive child. We need to study the "It" roles in different games so we may use this experience constructively in individual cases.

We should study the security needs of adolescents, and how effectively these needs are met by group activity in which patterns are clear-cut and definite: team games, group competition in apparatus, folk and square dance, drill teams and pep squads. There should also be studies of the effect of inventiveness and individual creativity in outdoor education, aquatics, creative dance, and the production of programs. Group direction and self-direction in ethical learnings should also be the subject of experimental investigation.

## Understanding movement

Human movement is the main business of physical education. Perhaps it is better to say that it is the means through which we work. Since we share the responsibility for teaching movement with no one else in the educational world, it behooves us to teach it effectively. This movement function of the human body is not limited to the traditional forms of physical education: sports, self-testing, games, and dance. It also appears in the course of everyday living as an expression of personality, as shown in Halsman's revealing photographs.[1] With this and other general aspects of movement, we need to work intensively.

Although all forms of physical education use movement, each has its own specialized approach. Each sport talks about and studies its specific skills: the lay-up shot in basketball, the bunt in baseball, the push pass in hockey, the back-hand in tennis. In most athletic sports the purpose of the specific skill is to control an object effectively. In track athletics the purpose is to control the body so as to get the greatest possible speed in running, distance or height in jumping. In adaptive physical education movement is designed to ameliorate handicaps of bodily build, habitual posture and carriage of the body. In figure skating, diving, gymnastics, and social dance, the purpose is to move in exact accordance with a prescribed pattern; in creative dance the purpose is to communicate, as in other forms of art. To accomplish such different purposes it is not surprising that we have developed different ways of talking about and of teaching specialized movements. As a general background for all this teaching we have used the study of

[1] *Philippe Halsman's Jump Book* (New York: Simon and Schuster, 1959).

body structure (anatomy), muscle function (physiology), joint and muscle action (kinesiology). Now we are beginning to question whether the traditional study of these separate sciences goes far enough in helping us to understand the general principles of good movement. We have become aware of the way experts in other fields are investigating movement: the industrialist through time-motion studies to conserve time and energy; the theatrical producer through training of gait and gesture to facilitate expression; the psychologist through considering movement as a projection, or overt expression, of personality. We are considering what we might learn from each other, and whether the application of holistic theory might not give leads we have failed to find in the more fragmented approach of specific movement analysis.

Artists and teachers of modern dance have started earlier and perhaps gone further than others in our field in attempting this total approach. They have identified and practiced such qualities of movement as focus, tempo, energy, use of space, and others. Several years ago a fruitful conference was held at the University of Wisconsin, attended by teachers of dance and teachers of sports. There was exchange of ideas on movement fundamentals; later courses were taught and a book was published on the subject.[2] Much of this material has been used at the college level in courses called basic skills or body mechanics. Since World War II the late Rudolph von Laban, teachers in his schools, and experts in elementary education in England have taught principles of weight, time, and space, to various age levels with conspicuous success.[3] Several American teachers and authors have applied general principles of movement to practical teaching programs and have written about them from the empirical or philosophical point of view.

[2] Ruth Glassow, *Fundamentals in Physical Education* (Philadelphia: Lea and Febiger, 1932).

[3] Ministry of Education, *Moving and Growing* and *Planning the Program* (London: Her Majesty's Stationery Office, 1952 and 1953).

English children in movement exploration

213

This all indicates a healthy interest in the more general and functional study of movement. It seems promising to use movement exploration in the elementary-school program and more definite movement education at the high-school and college level. As we work with program we should continue study of many of the unanswered questions. Is there transfer of control of quality of movement in general problems to control in the specific skills of sports and dance? What qualities of timing, application of energy or relaxation, and use of space are common to most sport skills? If a "common core" exists may it be taught in such a way as to facilitate learnings in different sports? Can a similar process be used in the physical skills of industry and agriculture? What about communication of emotion and ideas in the movement arts: dance and theatre? How may we use the team approach or interdisciplinary group methods in the solution of these problems?

## *Understanding competition*

Ours is a competitive society: at the same time it is highly co-operative. Games repeat this double relationship: competition between teams, co-operation within the team. The balance between co-operative and competitive activities in our program has always been a problem. To work intelligently at this problem we need much more background information about the social aspects of competition: what causes a culture to develop a competitive or co-operative pattern? [4] Do these patterns change in a given culture over a period of time? How do they affect the personality traits of individual members? Are there sex differences in competitive roles, i.e., are men expected to play a more competitive role than women—in our society? In other societies? We also need more specific information: what

---

[4] Margaret Meade, *Cooperation and Competition in Primitive Societies* (New York: McGraw-Hill, 1937).

different degrees of intensity in competition can be identified: in play, in school, in the home? What degree of intensity is advisable at different levels of maturity? For children of different temperaments? For optimum family living? What is the effect of competition on physiological stress? What degree of competition is necessary to obtain maximum performance or a high degree of excellence? What balance of competition and co-operation within a group makes for most effective group action? These and many other problems have immediate and crucial importance for teachers, recreation leaders, parents, management executives, and labor leaders, statesmen—in fact, for all persons dealing with humans in groups. Many of these questions may be approached by clinical methods, i.e., the case study rather than the normative or experimental method. Certainly sociologists, anthropologists, and psychologists should give resourceful help in this area of research.

### Temperamental differences in response to competition

*Courtesy Denver Public Schools Dept. of Health Edu.*

## Understanding fitness

When we talk about fitness today, we mean much more than strength and physical endurance. There is also a drive factor, partly psychological, partly moral. Call it will to win, courage, or what you will, it is vital to the full use of strength. Recent revelations of the behavior of many young American soldiers in Chinese prison camps showed astonishing weaknesses. One-fourth of them died, chiefly from lack of the will to go on living; they made no effort to escape; they informed on each other; they showed no group solidarity and little resistance to "brain-washing." [5] These young men were at the peak age of physical strength and they had all been through the army fitness programs, but they obviously lacked the moral stamina to make full use of their physical power.

We should know more about the interrelationship between different aspects of fitness. We need to study the environmental factors that caused our young soldiers to give up without a fight. We need to know how to stimulate some purpose for our work beyond strength. Youth can work harder, exercise with more effort over longer periods if they have a satisfactory answer to the questions "strength for what?" "endurance for what?" The immediate answer may be to win, if there is a team for *every* boy and *every* girl. It may be to win the admiration of their peer groups: fitness associated with good looks, a nice figure, pep, and skill for the girls; with muscular development, a man's skill and power for the boys.

Fitness for work may have no great appeal to youth, but to adult women and older men this may be an important consideration. As our economy expands to meet the demands of a growing population, as automation puts a premium on skilled rather than unskilled workers, these more mature persons may find it rewarding to return to the labor force. Whether or not

---

[5] Eugene Kinkead, *In Every War but One* (New York: Norton, 1959).

management is able to organize part-time schedules for them, mature workers will need to maintain work fitness. This poses a problem for adult education and community recreation agencies—setting up individualized programs of work and rest in a regime of gradual reconditioning. Many questions need to be studied before we can be fully effective in this kind of guidance. But beyond fitness for the purpose of winning a game, gaining admiration, or securing a job, we must somehow help youth to understand the importance of individual fitness in the survival of a free society. They must not only *know* but *feel* that in return for freedom they have obligations: to maintain the physical fitness (including mental and emotional maturity) that makes them good team members in any situation; and to use this total fitness gladly in the service of a free country.

## Building public understanding

What taxpayers do not know about physical education would fill a library. What they do know is that it costs money, wins (or loses—unforgivably) football and basketball games, and may have some relation to fitness. This is a situation that leaves us very vulnerable to current attacks on education. Just now these attacks follow the line that might be called "Back to the three R's" with science thrown in, of course, on account of Sputnik.

We need to study ways and means of telling the whole story of our work to parents and taxpayers in our community. It must be an honest story, based on the assumption that parents are interested in what their children are learning. We have assumed that parents must be entertained on a level as near that of TV, radio, and movie entertainment as we may approach. Consequently some schools have developed circuses and shows as part of their public relations programs. While these programs may entertain the crowd and even gratify the parents of stars, they offer no substantial answer to the charge that physical education is an expendable fad or frill. However, some schools have found a way to make the substantial answer by showing to parents children in the process of growth. They have made movies, had live television shows and radio discussions, and have held open house for visiting friends and parents. The best of these programs are given in a series, each concentrating on one phase of growth. For instance the development of ball handling skills and self-testing—all the way from six to eighteen years of age—makes an excellent sixty-minute program. Interest will be heightened if the program is followed by a question and discussion period. Another line of growth interesting to demonstrate, is intercultural understanding through participation in the games and dances of other countries.

At the college level "shows" are useful in a more limited way. Dance concerts and water ballets are good audience entertainment. To give understanding of the breadth of the modern college program TV may well be used, and student radio panels if well sparked by a good topic and a competent chairman.

Adult education and recreation agencies may best use mass media rather than audience demonstrations except for city-wide pageants and big participating events. Interesting topics could be the adult conditioning programs previously discussed, senior recreation programs, and the whole field of guidance in recreation budgeting. Average expenditures for recreation make up from 5 to 10 per cent of the family's budget, but the variability among different families is very great. Often the most satisfying recreational activities are the least expensive. For example, in suburbia most homes have yards large enough to make very fair playgrounds. To equip them with gym sets and trampolines is much more expensive and less developmental for the children than to improvise apparatus made and set up at home. An old bench or low table for climbing up and jumping down, a two-inch climbing rope securely fastened to a large tree, turning bars, well based in cement at two or three heights, will give much better returns for the investment. Often public resources for recreation are not known to newcomers in the neighborhood. Swimming pools, tennis courts, and even golf courses are provided by public agencies in some cities, as well as by private clubs. The difference in cost is very great, and it is useful for young families to have this information when budgeting recreation.

### Reassessment of values [6]

Underlying all of these problems is the fundamental question "What values in our society do we wish to emphasize?" Schools in a democracy have a double responsibility: to confirm existing social values, and to lead in reviving or developing others. According to some observers, values in our society have changed profoundly in the last generation. Riesman, and Whyte,[7] have described pressures toward conformity as pervading all phases and institutions of modern living. Lerner [8] illustrates the American character by describing personality types fairly common among us. Among them are the "neutral man," the "conformist," the "routineer," the "adjusting man . . . [who] just wants to merge into his social landscape, to offer as little exposed and vulnerable surface as possible to the storms of life, to take his place in the scheme of society with a minimum of effort and an economy of psychic hurt. This applies to his political behavior as it applies also to his behavior on his job, in his neighborhood, in his family, among his friends, and in his social set." These types have been molded

---

[6] "Value" is used here to mean what is considered worthwhile.

[7] David Riesman, Nathan Glazer, and Reuel Denney, *The Lonely Crowd* (New Haven: Yale University Press, 1950); and William Whyte, *The Organization Man* (New York: Simon and Schuster, 1956).

[8] Max Lerner, *America as a Civilization* (New York: Simon and Schuster, 1957), pp. 652–56. By permission.

by conformist pressures, others have not. Lerner describes some of the others as "the rebel," the "libertarian," the "committed American," and the "operational American" who carries out the creative impulse by getting a constructive job well done. Lerner concludes that no one of these portraits is more than a facet of the complex multiple personality that we call "American," that this multiple personality has changed and will change with changes in the social situation.

It is apparent that most of our program and method, traditional in physical education, has re-enforced pervading pressures toward conformity. To promote physical fitness we use mass exercises, prelearned and directed by the teacher. Almost always we conduct our games under set rules, with strategy thought up by the coach and learned by the players. In most types of dance the form of step and pattern is learned by rote, and even the mood of the dance is set as the teacher feels it. Stunts, track events, and ball handling skills are practiced as prescribed, and also apparatus exercises, swimming strokes, and dives.

On the other hand, schools that wish to foster constructive inquiry and invention, may do so with the same activities taught by a different approach. Even a program of calisthenics may be devised by a high-school or college student to meet his own individual needs. This must be done with the guidance of his instructor, after consulting the results of the student's tests. Information on what sets of muscles are weak, what defects of posture and feet may be helped by different types of exercises, what work-outs will improve endurance may be given by group guidance. The resulting set of exercises and training rules, as devised by the student, should be reviewed by the instructor, revised as necessary and well learned. This will give a more meaningful program that the student is much more likely to carry on after the pressure of school athletics is over.

Game strategy should be thought up by the players with the teacher's help. In the elementary school this may be done if the short huddle is introduced from time to time, and if the teacher asks pointed questions to develop the habit of out-guessing the opponent, of seeing the difference between offensive and defensive strategy, of thinking ahead of time and in the midst of play as well. In high-school and college situations, intramural programs and women's sports give more latitude for mistakes than varsity games. Even in the latter, however, as every coach knows, players must use their heads in carrying out a well-planned attack or defense. The author once saw a Phi Beta Kappa backfield man win a crucial game by the expedient of reversing the direction of a play well known to his own team and to the opponents. This was agreed to in the huddle: the resulting touchdown caught the opponents off balance, as well as both sets of coaches.

Steps and patterns of characteristic national dances are not invented nor revised by students or teachers. They are respected as traditional cultural forms. However, interpretation of the purpose and feeling of the dance should result from the class' own study of the national backgrounds that produced the dance. Creative rhythms and dance should be enjoyed at all age levels. More than any other form of physical education they give the opportunity for creative art experience with its outcomes of absorbed integration of all powers, all the talents of the group, and the release of effective expression. Movement exploration, an important preliminary to creative dance, and to sport skills, as well, calls for the child's own answer, through moving, to problems set by the teacher. It leads to an understanding and control of different qualities of movement and of the possibilities of his own physique that will help in performing sport skills as well as dance. In all forms of self-testing children will try to see what they can do, either with small equipment or on larger pieces of apparatus; how they can overcome obstacles; what new skills they can invent.[9]

9 Elizabeth Halsey and Lorena Porter, *Physical Education for Children* (New York: Henry Holt, 1958), Chaps. 10, 12.

What becomes of social adjustment when the inventive approach is used? As long as children work in groups they will be learning to adjust. When the group must solve its own problems, adjustment takes place at a higher level of effort and accomplishment than when their work is directed step by step. Third-graders who think up ways of making the "net" work together to catch the last lively "fish" are adjusting, as is a research "team" using the group method for defining and organizing work on an investigation. In both the procedure of respect for different opinions, and selection of one to try, is being learned. The level of complexity, of control, and of results is very different; training and experience at the simpler levels helps at all the other levels. At any level an entirely new approach or method may evolve from group thinking—cooperation has then re-enforced creativity.

Another value in our society is material wealth and ease of living as a means to happiness. This, say our economists, supports our entire industrial complex. Expectation of increasing demand for more goods and services, for more gadgets to make work easier and put comfort in living, keeps the wheels turning, money in circulation, and results in the highest (material) standard of living known by any country at any period in history. This value is held up as an ideal by "depth" advertising on television and radio. It exerts a cultural pressure against physical effort, discomfort, or hardship of any kind. It is, says the army, responsible for a generation of "softies" with more of them coming up through the schools at each graduation. The army takes a dim view of the chances for survival of "softies" when competing with troops of the have-not nations, used to hardship from birth. The pressure toward easy living puts teachers in a difficult position. Parents who are not successful in getting their children to work hard, expect the schools to do so. (But the work must not be too hard, children must not become fatigued nor be discouraged.) Effort toward excellence has been lost in modern school practice, say the authoritarians. Actually, of course, effort toward excellence has always been strengthened by purposes other than excellence for its own sake. Competition, recognition, social approval, as well as the individual student's wish to have and to use an excellent product, have been more potent than coercion, fear, or punishment.

It might seem that our whole program is in conflict with this cultural value. On the other hand, physical effort in itself is pleasurable to all healthy youngsters, most adolescents (boys more than girls) and adults in good condition (men more than women). Therefore we may consider as a not unattainable value, effort toward excellence rather than easy living, if we make the program "lively," as the children say, or "tough" in the language of adolescents. With the latter we should also emphasize the fact that it is something special to be able to take a tough program, and that while leading toward some of their own goals it also makes them feel good. Of course we should make sure of auxiliary purposes: competition for everyone through well-supervised intramurals and interscholastics, recognition through public programs and demonstrations in class, social approval by their peers and teachers for improvement as well as top performance. We hope they may adopt as their own, goals of increased strength, endurance, and skill. This is done naturally by the growing child. The adolescent and the young adult may be helped if they have the opportunity to learn activities of prestige value: golf, tennis, bowling, skating, skiing, and dance.

A specific example of effort or ease is offered by outdoor education taught in two ways. Camping may be done deluxe, or as the skilled woodsman prefers it, without extra trappings. In the deluxe camp a trip is usually an overnight affair, luggage is carried to the camp site by camp cars, while the campers get there by canoe or horseback. The guides pitch the tents, trench them, inflate the air mattresses, do the cooking and clean-up. Campers eat, put on a skit show, enjoy new scenery and possibly explore it a little after breakfast. Then they sit and make up a trip song, come back to main camp and regale them with the song and tales of their adventures in rugged outdoor living. In the woodsman's camp, on the other hand, all trips are carefully planned according to the age and experience of the small group selected; but even the small children on short overnights do most of the work. The older ones are proud of their efficiency on longer trips, involving more

work, taking equipment and supplies limited in weight and portable in form, menus simple but adequate. The campers learn how to stow their duffles to keep weight low in the canoes, how to portage, lean into packs, use available fuel and kindling for fires on safe or protected surfaces, cook mixes and dehydrated foods to make palatable meals, supplement them with berries found locally and identified as safe for eating, pitch

## Effort toward Excellence

*Department of Hygiene and Physical Edu. Wellesley College*

tents so as to stay dry, and the many other techniques of sufficiency by which the woodsman lives safely in the woods. Girls make as good campers as boys, both need well-trained counselors. Later on, when they have families of their own, alumni of the woodsman's camp can make family camping a satisfying and inexpensive vacation project.

Our moral values, based on Judaeo-Christian ethics, are often in conflict with the drive toward material success. However, there is evidence that religious belief, closely associated with democratic principles of human relationship, is increasing in influence. These principles are described at length and applied to physical education practice at different age levels in the first yearbook of our national organization.[10] In the author's opinion the most important part of a teacher's work is to know, to live, and to teach these values. Let us quote two of the principles described in the Yearbook:

1. *Human integrity comes first.* Humanity in oneself or others is always considered an end, never as a means to an end. . . . The coach of our football team refuses to take chances with his players; to him they are something more than a means to winning games. They have careful medical supervision, and the doctor's word is law. No boy plays without unqualified medical approval. Coach Brown considers the boy's future health more important than any game at any stage of the season.

Sue is a likable, charming student. She knows how to use her charm to raise her grade point average. She is relying more and more on personality, less and less on work, so her own very fine mind will probably never be developed. She does not respect humanity in herself.

10. *Sportsmanship is applied religion.* Church and home alike tell the child that he is his brother's keeper, that he should treat others as he wants to be treated. This basic concept becomes the living spirit of the game whenever opponents treat

---

[10] *Developing Democratic Human Relations* (Washington: AAHPER, 1951), pp. 354–59. By permission.

each other with respect, recognize that each side has the same right to a well-played, spirited game, promoting the best performance of each team and each player.

This principle is violated by the coach or player who deliberately sets out to undermine the opponent's morale or self-control. Spectators will more often do this than either coach or players. In this case a thousand fans can be wrong, and the conformist or the neutralist in the crowd will be just as wrong.

### Education for change

Rapid change is characteristic of our age. We cannot always foresee the direction of change, but it is possible to equip students to deal with change. Let small children change unworkable rules of a game by general discussion and concensus; help adolescents to make constructive changes in procedures of their extracurricular organizations and programs; teach college youth and research students to be critical in reviewing literature that bears on problems of concern to them. The following criteria have been applied to scientific attitudes, basic to education for change: [11]

a. Are students alert to differences and changes in persons and situations?

b. Are they ready to challenge authority, to experiment, to test tradition by their own experience?

c. Do they ask specific, significant questions, and obtain all relevant facts?

d. Do they keep open minds, considering impartially all available facts, and then reason out the best answers available to them at that time?

e. Do they consider these answers as qualified and limited by their own points of view, rather than as universal truths?

---

[11] *Ibid.*, p. 359.

f.   Are they ready to act on the basis of these answers although they recognize them as tentative and subject to continuous review?

Bernice and Harry Moore have put this well: [12]

> Education today is education for growing, changing, developing. It is education for flexibility. It is not so much training in the subject matter itself as in the ways of obtaining what we need as time goes on. We need teachers with imagination and creativity; teachers need to teach with these qualities and attempt to develop them in students.

What about the enduring values, the basic principles of religious belief and democratic procedures? How balance stability with the need for change? Historical perspective is helpful. As early as we teach traditional games and dances of other cultures, we also teach that they have developed over a long period of time and characterize the way other peoples have lived. In our own culture there also are games and dances expressive of periods in our own history. These we recognize and keep in their social context. So we may help even elementary school children to respect enduring ways of dance and play. More permanent, and of course more significant are the enduring values of ethical conduct that we have just been discussing. For thousands of years, and in many cultures the validity of these moral truths has been tested. They govern even small details of our procedure. When we open the privilege of participation in games and sports to all without racial, religious, or any other discrimination; when we accept the discipline of sportsmanlike conduct to opponents as well as to teammates, we are fulfilling a deep demand of our cultural inheritance. We cannot deny this demand with impunity.

---

[12] National Conference of DGWS and NAPECW, *Social Changes & Sport* (Washington: AAHPER, 1959), p. 65.

## QUESTIONS

1. Illustrate what is meant by the terms "withdrawn" and "overaggressive" children. Have you ever seen any?

2. Have you ever been in a group that planned and put on a program? What creative talents were called forth? From whom?

3. Can you think of two general skills common to baseball, basketball, and hockey? Skills common to archery and golf? Swimming and dance?

4. What competitive situations, aside from sports, exist in college? Are they a help or hindrance to most students? List them in order of intensity.

5. Have you watched young children under intense competition? How does it affect children of different temperaments? Withdrawn children? Aggressive children?

6. What competition does your father have to meet in his business? Does your mother have to compete with other persons?

7. Can you give illustrations from campus life of situations in which the ethical imperative is well-observed? Ignored or violated?

8. Plan a daily regime of exercise, work, study, sleep, food, and recreation that would improve your fitness (a week's program). Would the same kind of program improve the fitness of a woman of fifty? A man of twenty-one?

9. What questions about fitness would you ask a doctor or an authority in physiology? Make a list.

10. Give examples of good and poor sportsmanship you have observed this fall: a) at football games; b) in intramurals.

11. In your church youth group get reactions to the statement we have made: "Good sportsmanship is applied religion." Bring a report back to class.

12. Are there any forms of discrimination in your own home town? In this college community? Plan a panel discussion on this topic for your major club: Be sure to have students on the panel representing both sexes, minority groups, and different fields of study.

## SELECTED REFERENCES

Glassow, Ruth. *Fundamentals in Physical Education* (Philadelphia: Lea and Febiger, 1932), Sections I and II.

*Philippe Halsman's Jump Book* (New York: Simon and Schuster, 1959).

Ministry of Education. Chap. I in *Moving and Growing* and Chap. VI in *Planning the Program* (London: Her Majesty's Stationery Office, 1952).

*National Conference on Social Changes and Implications for Physical Education and Sports Programs* (Washington: AAHPER, 1959), pp. 35–57, 71–96.

*Report on Essentials of Physical Education for Youth International Congress Connecticut Valley Colleges* (Washington: AAHPER, 1955), pp. 14–19.

Wessel, Janet. *Movement Fundamentals* (Englewood Cliffs: Prentice-Hall, 1957), Chaps. VI–VII.

# CHAPTER 9

# *Unfinished Business:*

## YOUR PART

REMEMBER HIGH-SCHOOL graduation exercises? Hot auditorium—platform flowers—worried teachers—proud parents—seniors cleaned up and dressed up, edgy under the too-casual surface—background music—the invocation suddenly more serious than church—and then the speaker. Clever or dull, understanding or remote, that man told you to go about saving the world. Nine chances out of ten, before he had finished, you wondered why he and the other brass hats, so much ·more experienced and capable than your crowd, hadn't done the job themselves, and given you all a decent world to live in. What you really wanted was a stable society where things stayed put, where you had a definite place and knew what to do with yourselves. Now if you had been an adolescent in a primitive tribe of the South Sea Islands you might have had it. Your initiation into adulthood, by solemn and perhaps painful rites, would have put you into a situation where you knew just what to do. Tribal rules told you just how to fight, to fish, to plant, to take a mate and raise a family. No problems, no difficult decisions for the individual . . . and no horizons.

However, you had the luck to be born in a complex society in which a high-school youth grows up slowly. You have a great deal of freedom and many responsibilities not always very clearly defined. You have, in addition, the luck to be in college so you may learn to make more intelligent use of freedom. (It was not a college graduate who gave up his job sorting potatoes, saying "Decisions, decisions, nothing but decisions!") Yes, you have the luck to grow through making decisions, in an open society, and in a changing and growing profession. In this chapter we shall discuss your part in the future growth of our profession, your responsibility in undertaking some phase of the unfinished business ahead.

## New opportunities

Every one of the problems discussed in the previous chapter is more than a task. Each presents the opportunity for many kinds of constructive work. Some one of you, for instance, is going to find out the balance between cooperation and competition best for nine-year-olds playing beat ball. Some one of you may study the motor learning of a group through childhood and adolescence. Some one of you is going to write the script and plan the action for a television show that will be used nationally to show training for democracy through basketball for high-school girls. Some one is going to be on a team of research workers studying the role of movement in release of stress; perhaps another of that team will consult with management in setting up a study of movement useful in situations of industrial tension.

Not merely more and better teaching, physical therapy, and recreation jobs are ahead, but a greater need for planning and thinking through studies in many crucial areas. As a guide to such study you will need a working philosophy of physical education.

## *Exploring a new philosophy*

When you feel like saying "so what" to any statement you hear from an instructor, you are really saying something about your own philosophy. The speaker's statement has no operational effect on you. That is, it doesn't move you to action one way or another. For you it does not have value. For example if you value grades only, not use of things you learn, you just don't listen when your instructor gets off the required topic. The minute he begins "For those of you who wish to explore the learning theory further," your ears close, your mind says "so what" and although you may present an admirable picture of courteous attention, no notes are taken, no words register until he goes on with "Now to return to the third point in the outline."

These values of yours, then, are your philosophy. Science measures, philosophy interprets and evaluates. For the rest of your life you'll be increasing your store of facts ascertained by science or experience. As you organize these facts you'll develop a pattern that takes account of facts, values, and purposes. The pattern will point toward certain actions, away from others. For instance you hear or read a report: an experimental training program produced significant results in improved fitness of a group of college women, by fifteen-minutes exercise daily for a period of one month. Retest showed retention of results for only two weeks after exercise was discontinued. This information will be absorbed into your philosophy according to your values. If you believe that humans work best under self-direction you'll explore every possible means of motivating girls and women in your classes to plan, learn, and do their own set of exercises, and test themselves from time to time on the results. If you believe that effort such as this results only from outside discipline, you'll try to motivate girls and women to enjoy fitness classes and to enroll them in the Y.W.C.A.

During your professional course you'll be establishing your

philosophy of physical education. By the time you are a senior some one is going to ask you to state it: an instructor, a classmate, or a school superintendent in a job interview. Many others along the way will challenge you as to what this field is all about. So it's best to be as clear about it as you can as soon as you can. To begin with, you must select values for yourself, for your own action. Look again at the discussion of values in the preceding chapter. How do you evaluate conformity and creativity? How do you find satisfaction for yourself? In terms of comforts? Status? Service? Happiness? What facets of the American character described by Lerner serve you as a theme for living? Have you a better term than any of these to describe your own pattern? What of our basic beliefs in human relationship? Three ways of expressing these beliefs are deeply respected in our culture. Which do you accept? Which serves you best as a guide to conduct? Is there any fundamental difference in their meaning? They are:

> The Golden Rule: Matthew 7:12
> The Ethical Imperative: Kant
> Reverence for Life: Albert Schweitzer

What general goals in teaching are based on the values in living you are working out for yourself?

Your philosophy will begin with values (from which your goals are derived). You will continually add facts and generalized truths based on facts (principles). Then will come general lines of conduct (policies) and specific ways of teaching, learning, and acting in daily living (practice). If you can organize all this: what you believe in, what you are aiming at, what you know, and what you do, into a related pattern, you'll have a better chance for consistency and less danger of frustration and inner conflict than if you make no such effort.

This improvement in integration of your powers will help you to contribute to the growth of our profession. Your contribution may be important even as an undergraduate; it will be of greater importance as you grow in experience and wisdom—as a graduate student, a teacher, a parent, and homemaker. Does it all seem too difficult? Do you feel with the small girl called "Fatty" Peck who said at the age of five: "I'm never going to learn *A* because then I'll have to learn *B*!"?

## Contributions to unfinished business

Undergraduates are nearer to adolescents in point of time than the rest of us, and so can better understand them. A youngster in her first year of senior high school said she wanted to teach in junior high some day, because "they have so many problems, and no one understands them." Remembering your own experiences from twelve years on and observing young persons of the same ages from a more analytical viewpoint than formerly, you might note your opinions on these points:

1. Do they like prescribed routines: calisthenics, pep squad drills, definite steps and figures in dances, or do they like to make up their own?

2. When they adopt constitutions or plan programs do they want to start from scratch, i.e., without adult help or finding out what other teenage groups have done? Do they get easily confused by this procedure? How do they get things done?

3. If you have ever been a part of a teenage group or class that made up a code of behavior, try to recall the steps taken and the points they decided on.

As undergraduates you may study movement by your own experiences in major activity courses. For example, try to apply to sports what you learn in dance about the use of energy and relaxation, timing, and direction. Analyze the rhythmic pattern of your own running front dive and compare it with the pattern of the best diver you have ever seen, in the same event. In regard to competition, you might list the competitive situations that have already occurred in your living unit, and try to distinguish those that are most intense from those that are least intense. Do the same thing with high-school experiences you remember, both in class work and extracurricular activities. Do the same with all college sports. When you go home for the weekend or your next vacation, try to put yourself in the place of your youngest brother or sister and feel what competitive pressures he or she meets. What co-operation exists in the family situation?

In connection with the problem of fitness, talk to any of the men you know who have had experience in Chinese prison camps. Do they agree with the Kinkead report? How do they account for weak morale on the part of American prisoners? Have you any information about your own fitness? Do you think you have more or less endurance than when you began your college work? Do you get more or less sleep than when you were in high school? More or less exercise? Do you think physical education majors in your school are more or less fit than other college students? Are they improving more or less than other students in this respect? It would be a good idea to think carefully about other problems our profession must meet, in addition to these we have been discussing. As an undergraduate you are keeping files with teaching material from all your classes. In your files you might make a section on professional problems, in which you keep your notes, your observations, your questions, and your thinking on these matters. Even if you do not have the answers now, you will be contributing. Your experience is valuable to others, and so are your questions. Of great value to yourself is the process of reflective thinking and looking about for ways to find answers.

Graduate students, of course, are expected to make more specialized contributions. On the Ph.D. level the dissertation is supposed to contribute by digging out (not just digging) and reporting facts not already available. Before working on any particular question, however, the investigator must know something of the background. That is, he should first select the area in which his problem lies, and plan his graduate courses so he may feel more familiar with this area. For instance, in addition to graduate courses and undergraduate specialization in physical education, these other courses will help:

Understanding children and youth—child development, psychology, physical growth, sociology.
Understanding competition—sociology and anthropology.
Understanding movement—anatomy, kinesiology, correctives, psychology, dance, sports, theater, industrial management.
Understanding fitness—physiology of exercise, endocrinology, psychology, gymnastics, sports, dance.

Techniques of research used by the graduate student will vary with the problem. This is not the appropriate place to elaborate on methods to be used in the investigation of problems. However, a real contribution is more likely to result if the graduate student works in an area of vital interest to him, and plans subsequent as well as degree studies. All of his studies may then be brought together in a published report or book of value to other advanced students.

The teacher may contribute in many ways, even if very busy with classes. Some teachers, before accepting a position, have had an understanding with the superintendent permitting them to do some experimental teaching, systematic observation, or other kind of study while teaching. In a very large and conservative school system this is not always feasible, but smaller schools in modern-minded communities are often glad to have such projects carried on. The special teacher of physical education in the elementary school is in an excellent position to carry on longitudinal studies. He may, for instance, measure some motor skill with the same children over a period of years. Or, if money is available for tape recording, make continuing studies of group adjustment. Anecdotal records, sociograms, and other sociometric techniques will yield useful data if planned within a sound research structure. Help in setting up

Competition can be serious business

Competition is fun

the problem is available, of course, to teachers who have begun their graduate work in summer sessions. In this case on-the-job research is a definite, accredited part of the degree program. Post degree research is also important. Team projects are very useful to research investigators in a neighboring center of learning, and often foundation or other funds may be tapped to provide equipment and statistical help.

Mothers and homemakers may also continue their professional interests and make many contributions to our unsolved problems. We have pointed out in Chapter 3 that women who have majored in health, physical education or recreation are especially well equipped to bring up children because of their basic science training, their studies pertinent to child health, their understanding of child development, and their practical knowledge of valuable recreation and physical education activities for the whole family.

Recently the college-trained wife and mother has been described as a frustrated soul, weeping for lost opportunities as she loads the duomatic. This author puts little stock in such descriptions, sees no necessity for feelings of frustration, and knows many buoyant young women who accomplish much for their communities as well as for their families, being efficient in the daily round of multitrivia. Aside from the fact that a major in these fields uses her college training continuously for her family, there are seven (or more) ways in which she may continue to grow, and, in turn, contribute to the growth of our profession:

1.  By muscle training through bath play, pushing against the baby's legs or arms, letting him pull up while holding on to her hands, putting toys where he will roll over or sit up to get them. This is fun for both; in addition the mother should note the amount of time the child wants activity, the effect on his growth, appetite, and sleep.

2.  By systematic observation and noting details of develop-

ment of motor skills such as climbing and supporting weight, getting up and down from chairs, sofas, etc.; natural and taught techniques of climbing down, and jumping down; inventing stunts on play apparatus; inventing skills with balls.

3. By systematic observation and noting skills of group adjustment: sharing playthings and parallel play; first signs of co-operative play when each may do something in relation to what the other is doing; play in larger groups with more organized co-operation.

4. Keeping a record of home accidents, and the child's caution in preventing accidents.

5. Seeking advice and direction in making observations, either from child development authorities in the nearest University or from alumnae conferences and workshops for married graduates.

6. Organizing study groups in PTA to draw up criteria for good school physical education programs, and to observe and evaluate those local programs they find available.

7. Continued subscription to the *Journal of Health, Physical Education and Recreation,* asking for section meetings for homemakers at conferences, stressing importance of using physical education graduates who are homemakers as public relations channels.

Most of these methods of study apply to the first problem: understanding children and youth. They may be used equally well on any of the other problems. Certainly married graduates are in a strategic position to build public understanding and support of good local programs, and they will wish to keep up with the changes in their departments in the alma mater institution to check on education for change.

In contributing to the future of our profession, married alumnae will be contributing to their own futures. To most of the readers of this book the time when they'll be in their own home seems remote enough. Those later days when the children are grown, the house is empty, and the main part of the mother's job is done, seem too far away to be interesting. But look around at the middle-aged women of your acquaintance. Which are the happy ones: the occupied or the idle, those who have a multitude of vital interests, or those who have a scarcity? You may build your own happiness and competence for the middle years by continuing your professional growth while the children are small. There will be some sort of paid position or some important community responsibility waiting for the mature woman who has kept growing, who is alert and in working trim.

## Evaluating college as an investment

The cost of a college education is not met by tuition and fee payments, even in expensive private institutions. Society foots much of the bill through taxes, endowments, gifts, and scholarships. Both democratic and totalitarian governments recognize the value of higher education in returns to society. The difference is in the relative freedom of the individual to choose whether or not he will go to college. In our country the individual has this freedom—if he also has the money, or the opportunity to earn his way and scholastic aptitude. It is important, then, for each of you to evaluate college costs in terms of the returns for you and the probable returns to society. In general, the many studies that have been made comparing the incomes of graduates and nongraduates in relation to the over-all costs of going to college, report that the financial returns on the investment for the individual are good, if considered over a period of years: the status returns definitely positive; and the personal satisfactions also favor college study. Is college a good investment for every young person of college age? Of course not. Ability to profit by college study exists in only part of the college age group. How large a part depends somewhat on the available accommodations and objectives of the college. At this time we may expect entrance requirements to become more restrictive, since college enrollments are increasing more rapidly than the financial resources of the colleges.

You have already met entrance requirements, and you are now in a position to estimate your success, and to answer the question: can I continue with profit to society, the college, my family, and myself? It may help in this estimate to ask yourself a few questions:

Is a college education essential to my life goals?

Am I increasingly interested in preparing for physical education, health education, physical therapy, or recreation leadership as a profession?

Am I able to meet the standards of the college and the department in my work?

If not can I analyze my own difficulties: study habits? organization of work within time for work? getting along with other students? with faculty? can I get expert help from college counselors or departmental advisers?

Will my money hold out? How much can I earn next summer? Are there scholarships for which I might apply? Part time jobs in this community? Loan funds? Any other sources?

Have I good rapport with my adviser? Will she help me plan a developmental program that would include personal growth as well as professional preparation? Am I willing to work at both of these lines of development? Am I willing to try to live on a schedule?

Am I learning about the rich resources of this campus in out-of-class as well as in-class learnings? Do libraries, lectures, concerts, plays, social contacts, sports, dances, various organizations attract (but not distract) me? Do I try to balance or harmonize work and play, exercise and rest, human relations and religious faith?

After asking yourself all these serious questions and thinking about the answers as they apply to your own abilities and future actions, it is probably time to make decisions. Then forget your own self-evaluation, enjoy your friends, listen to their problems and think of what help they need. There is no greater bore than the person who takes himself too seriously, talks and thinks only of himself, and works only for himself. An occasional session of self-evaluation is healthy; a habit of self absorption is very poor mental hygiene, and very poor entertainment! Most of you are fortunate enough to be outgoing and activity-minded. Therefore you have no great tendency toward self-centered introspection, and it will be of no help to develop such a tendency.

### Planning now

If you are sure that college will be a good investment for you—and no loss to society—it will be interesting to look ahead and make plans for your future development in the profession. There are several possibilities depending on your interests.

If you wish to specialize in two or three activities the line of work and training might go like this: high school teaching, with summers spent in special camps or summer schools where there is expert instruction in your sport. After three or four years of this, then a year of graduate study in which you will have advanced activity courses and lecture courses that will help you understand how people learn. When you have completed requirements for an M.A. degree you'll be ready to teach your activities (and probably others) in a college or large high school. For further progress you will want to do some research and writing.

Procedure will differ somewhat if you are interested in teaching children. An elementary school position would start you off, and playground leadership or camp counseling would be good experience for the summer. Soon you might be planning summer study, and then a year in residence at some college for your Master's. You would look for a University or Teachers'

College that had good graduate work in physical education with some strong courses in elementary physical education, child development, and elementary education. You would want an opportunity to see a first-rate campus school in action. After you had completed work for your Master's degree, there would be opportunities to teach in more responsible elementary positions leading up to city supervisory work, or in teacher training departments in a college or University. There you might eventually give lecture courses on methods, and coordinate and supervise major students' experiences in laboratory teaching. After further study and a doctor's degree the road would be wide open as far as your ability and interest could take you.

If dance is your field, you will need a background of high-school teaching experience. Also you will find many interesting possibilities for study as you teach. In a metropolitan center there may be an excellent opportunity for studio lessons with some dance artist or well-known teacher. If modern dance is not available, try some ballet. The skills, discipline, and experience will be valuable, though you will probably never want to teach it—certainly not to children. In the summer numerous dance courses are given. Make a list of these while still in college. Read the news notes from the dance section in the journal, and advertisements of dance offerings in different summer schools. Read the dance magazine, and consult with your own and other dance teachers for evaluation of the work you find mentioned in these sources. Study and practice in the related arts: theater, music, graphic and plastic arts, design, and literature. Get all the production experience you can. If you can organize your work toward the master's degree it will be helpful in getting a college position. In most colleges you will be expected to teach other activities in addition to dance. Follow your interest here, and prepare yourself in two or three sports, movement education, gymnastics, or adaptive work. Your advancement with this preparation will depend on your ability as a teacher, readiness to work with the rest of the staff, and to understand and work for general departmental aims and programs. The production efforts of your dance group and your contribution to building favorable community relationships will have a great deal to do with your success. If you can become an artist in teaching as well as in performance, in human relations as well as in dance production, there will be a wide horizon ahead.

If you are a recreation major it will also be best to plan a sequence of experience, study, and experience at a higher level of responsibility. These plans will depend on your job interests. If it is to be community recreation then summer experience on playgrounds, or as a camp counselor, will be very helpful even during your college course. Your job will, of course, be a year-round position, and when you want to study you will have to get a leave of absence. If you are working in a metropolitan area there may be some local University that offers graduate work; if not in recreation it may be in one of the related areas such as sociology or social welfare. Your mornings may be free enough to give time for a course or two, but study will have to be done in the morning also, since you will be on the job in the evenings. If you plan to specialize in hospital recreation it would be a very good idea to work as a nurses' aid during some summer so you see the hospital from the inside, and get some knowledge of patients' psychological needs.

If you are a health education major, you may get your first experience teaching health and other subjects. Your summer study should follow lines indicated by your developing interests. If you stay in school work you will want courses that keep you in touch with recent developments in the school health program and supervisory techniques. If you become interested in public health work you will need additional training in a large area of study. However, public health positions are usually year-round jobs, so that a formal program of graduate study depends on securing leave of absence. In all branches of the health field there are opportunities for extension courses, workshops, conferences, and other forms of inservice training. This is especially true if your interest takes you into work with national organizations such as the American Red Cross, the National Tuberculosis Association, and the Foundation for Infantile Paralysis. If you decide to go into physical therapy, you might think first of work as a therapist in a doctor's office, in a clinic, or in a hospital. This experience will give the necessary practical basis for later supervision or teaching positions. In most schools a year of concentrated graduate study is necessary before entrance into the field.

In all of these plans, teaching children or adolescents immediately after graduation, before beginning graduate work, is stressed. The value of this experience has already been discussed,[1] and will not be repeated now. It is underlined here, because in this author's opinion the understanding of children and youth that comes from teaching them in a school situation is indispensable. It will improve your own teaching ability in any situation, it will be needed when you teach future teachers, and it will help you in your own family living later on.

Plans for your teaching should be based on the expectation of promotion as you have more experience and graduate study. However, you should not plan to move from one job to another too frequently. It's an old saying with school men that in her first year a young teacher is a liability because she has so much to learn and needs so much supervisory help. In her second year she is breaking even, in her third and subsequent years she is really contributing without handicaps. When your papers are reviewed, as those of an applicant for any position, one year stands will raise a question in the minds of those selecting among candidates—unless it is a one-year graduate assistantship. A record of constructive work in one position over a period of years speaks more clearly than any nice sounding

[1] See Chapter 4.

recommendation. The latter may readily be obtained because it is much easier for a kindly disposed administrator to write than a more realistic appraisal of strong and weak points.

Of course, as Robert Burns put it many years ago:

> The best laid plans of mice and men
> Gang aft agley.

Your plans may be "best laid" and may be interrupted. Probably they will be interrupted by marriage, and certainly this is a very excellent outcome all around. Even so, as we have just been saying, this may change the direction of your professional plans, but it does not need to put them on the shelf. Married or single, you may still contribute significantly to a profession that has already accomplished much, and needs your help to accomplish more.

## QUESTIONS

1. Write, briefly and as clearly as you can, your philosophy of physical education (or health or recreation) as of today.
2. Write out your plan for the next ten years as you see it today.

## SELECTED REFERENCES

Doane, C. J., P. J. VanderLinden, B. E. David, M. A. Bunson, and P. K. Vonk. *Introduction to College* (Boston: Allyn and Bacon, 1958), Pt. V.

Oberteuffer, Delbert. *Physical Education* (New York: Harper, 1951), Chap. X.

# *Appendix A*

AAHPE    American Association for Health and Physical Education (This was the title of our national organization 1937–38)

AAHPER    American Association for Health, Physical Education, and Recreation (This is present title since 1938–39)

ACHO    American Child Health Organization

APEA    American Physical Education Association (The title of our national association from 1903 to 1937)

BNSG    Boston Normal School of Gymnastics

CAPECW    Central Association for Physical Education of College Women

DGWS    Division of Girls' and Women's Sports

GAA    Girls' Athletic Association

NAAF    (Women's Division) National Amateur Athletic Federation

NAPECW    National Association for Physical Education of College Women

NCAA    National Collegiate Athletic Association

NCATE    National Council for Accreditation of Teacher Education

NEA    National Education Association

NSWA    National Section on Women's Athletics (Now DGWS)

PTA    Parent Teachers' Association (Formal title: National Congress of Parents and Teachers)

WAS    Women's Athletic Section (Changed to NSWA, then to DGWS)

WCOTP    World Congress of Organizations for Teacher Preparation

Y.M.C.A.    Young Men's Christian Association

Y.W.C.A.    Young Women's Christian Association